edexcel
advancing learning, changing lives

Literacy
Teacher's Handbook
Level 2

Alan Pearce

A PEARSON COMPANY

Consultants **Geoff Barton** and **Muriel Lloyd Lavery**

Published by:
Edexcel Limited
One90 High Holborn
London
WC1V 7BH
www.edexcel.org.uk

Distributed by:
Pearson Education Limited
Edinburgh Gate
Harlow
Essex
CM20 2JE
www.longman.co.uk

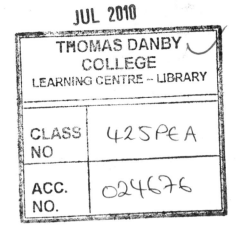

First published 2006
Fifth impression 2009

ISBN   978-1-84690-138-6

Edited and typeset by Ken Vail Graphic Design
Cover and text design by Ken Vail Graphic Design
Cover image Photos.com
Printed and bound in Great Britain at 4edge Limited, Hockley

The publisher's policy is to use paper manufactured from sustainable
forests.

⊚ Practice Tests CD

This CD was produced as a successor to the DfES Move On project 2003–6.
The test questions within the CD carry Crown copyright. Details of the
Move On programmes, commissioned by LSIS, can be found at
www.move-on.org.uk.

Acknowledgements
The Publisher would like to thank all schools involved in research into
this book.

The Publisher is grateful to all the copyright owners whose material
appears in this book. Every effort has been made to trace the copyright
holders and we apologise in advance for any unintentional omissions.
We would be pleased to insert the appropriate acknowledgement in any
subsequent edition of this publication.

Contents

Introduction: getting the best from Adult Literacy and Adult Numeracy

The Adult Literacy Level 2 Skills Book and Teacher's Handbook

This Teacher's Handbook and accompanying Skills Book have been designed to provide everything you need to teach Level 2 Adult Literacy successfully – whether you are an experienced practitioner or are embarking on the teaching of literacy for the first time.

The materials provided in the Skills Book and the Teacher's Handbook are designed to be **flexible**, suitable for teaching an individual, a group or the whole class. Although written with schools primarily in mind, these books are equally valuable in a college or work-based setting.

The primary purpose of these books is to make the teaching and learning process **as easy and as effective as possible**. To this end, all the skills required to meet the demands of the test have been carefully explained in a way that is understandable to a young person, with exercises specifically devised to reflect what the test requires.

There is freedom for you to cover the sections of the book in the order which suits your students, and you can concentrate on their identified areas of weakness using the wide range of exercises and test materials provided, including the Practice Tests CD-ROM provided with this Teacher's Handbook, and the Hot Topics CD-ROM included with the Skills Book which gives motivating games and activities to help students enjoy practising essential skills.

Each section of the Handbook has **two pages of guidance** on how to teach the skills required. Based on the tried and tested ideas of experienced teachers, these pages will help you teach effectively and in a lively and meaningful way.

Each section contains additional **photocopiable material** to help students gain confidence as they master the skills. To give students more practice before moving on, **six pages of photocopiable material per section** reinforce initial learning by providing exercises similar to those they have already encountered in their Skills Book. This allows for flexibility in teaching, meeting the needs of individuals as well as entire classes.

Progress is easily monitored on the **tracking grid** provided and a photocopiable **certificate** is included to record the completion of the course. **Answers to all questions are included**, along with suggestions for further practice if students have struggled with

particular types of question. A further **nine sample tests** are included on the accompanying Practice Tests CD-ROM for additional testing, and this can be used both for revision and practice, and to get students used to doing the tests on computer.

The response of both students and teachers in pre-publication trials has been entirely positive. We hope you enjoy using the materials, and wish you and your students every success!

The Adult Literacy and Adult Numeracy qualifications

The Level 2 Literacy qualification is one of four Adult Literacy and Adult Numeracy qualifications:

- Adult Literacy Level 1
- Adult Literacy Level 2
- Adult Numeracy Level 1
- Adult Numeracy Level 2.

These are all test-only qualifications with no portfolio, but the same tests are used for Adult Literacy and Adult Numeracy and for Key Skills Communication and Application of Number (see chart on page 10). This means that students can:

- move on to a Key Skills qualification by completing a portfolio
- still gain a qualification if they start Key Skills but don't complete a portfolio.

There is a charge for transferring between qualifications, but students receive a certificate upon passing the test and portfolio.

There are **significant advantages** to teaching Adult Literacy and Adult Numeracy in schools. Students who would formerly have left school with few qualifications have the opportunity to achieve **accreditation and success** while schools experience an improvement in their threshold position in the Achievement and Accreditation Tables.

Adult Literacy and Adult Numeracy increase **student motivation** and provide a more favourable assessment method for those who find difficulty with traditional examinations. Young people can justifiably feel a real sense of achievement as they gain certification which meets employer needs.

Adult Literacy and Adult Numeracy qualifications can also **contribute to GCSE achievement**. Adult Literacy and Adult Numeracy Level 1 are each worth 12.5 points. Each Level 2 is worth 23 points. This compares with Short Course GCSE Grade E 14 points and Grade B 23 points.

Adult Literacy and Numeracy Tests	Key Skills qualification	GCSE	GNVQ	NVQ
Level 1	Level 1	D–G grade	Foundation	Level 1
Level 2	Level 2	A*–C grade	Intermediate	Level 2

Schools benefit from an improved position on the **Achievement and Attainment Tables** as each Adult Literacy and Adult Numeracy qualification contributes 10% towards threshold.

"We offer Adult Literacy and Numeracy to our Year 11 pupils and 64% achieved both at Level 2 making a 2% difference to our Level 2 threshold on the Achievement and Attainment Tables. These qualifications have made a significant improvement in our average point scores where Adult Literacy and Numeracy were in the best eight qualifications listed. We intend to enter every pupil for these tests next year and are very pleased that we are offering them at our school."

Jeff Sturrock, Assistant Head Teacher,
Biddick Sports College.

The test

The tests can be taken either on paper (12 opportunities per year) or on-screen (any day, any time), and the same items are used for both paper-based and on-screen tests. There are also Entry Level qualifications available as paper-based tests.

There are 40 questions and all are multiple choice. The Literacy test lasts 1 hour (Numeracy, 1 hour 15 minutes) and instant provisional results are provided at the end of the test. If the result is a pass, papered results (Individual Results Notice or IRN) and a certificate are issued within ten working days. There is no limit to the number of times a student can sit a test, although a fee is payable for every test taken.

Detailed results feedback is available through Edexcel Online (www.edexcelonline.co.uk). For more information, contact the Edexcel Online Customer Support Team on 0870 240 9819.

More support from Edexcel

The Skills for Life team provides regular email updates and centre support packs. The Edexcel Information Manual provides information about administration arrangements. See www.edexcel.org.uk/sfc/emp-tp/infomanual/keyskills.

You can get further support for implementing the qualification from Edexcel.

- Website: www.edexcel.org.uk
- Email: skillsforlife@edexcel.org.uk
- Telephone: 0870 240 9800
- Regional Support: salessupport@edexcel.org.uk.

Other resources

There is a wide range of learning materials available from many websites. For example:

- Basic Skills Agency: www.basic-skills.co.uk
- Readwrite plus: www.dfes.gov.uk/readwriteplus
- Design your own practice tests: www.itembank.org.uk
- BBC Skillswise: www.bbc.co.uk/skillswise.

Coverage of national standards

The chart below indicates how the sections of the Skills Book map across to the national standards for reading and writing. For details of coverage of speaking and listening, see the charts at the beginning of each section in this book.

Standard	Skills Book Section	Skills Book page	Teacher's Handbook Section and page
Rt: Reading comprehension			
Rt2.1 trace and understand main events of continuous descriptive, explanatory and persuasive texts	A1: Skimming, scanning and close reading A3: Finding main points and details C2: Understanding descriptive texts C3: Understanding explanation texts C4: Understanding persuasive texts	4 10 30 34 38	
Rt2.2 identify purpose of a text and infer meaning which is not explicit	A1: Skimming, scanning and close reading B1: How information texts are organised C1: Identifying audience and purpose C2: Understanding descriptive texts C3: Understanding explanation texts C4: Understanding persuasive texts C5: Understanding argument texts and identifying points of view C6: Understanding formal and informal texts	4 16 26 30 34 38 42 46	B: page 32 C: page 40
Rt2.3 identify main points and specific detail	A1: Skimming, scanning and close reading A3: Finding main points and details	4 10	A: page 24
Rt2.4 read an argument and identify points of view	C4: Understanding persuasive texts C5: Understanding argument texts and identifying points of view	38	
Rt2.5 read critically to evaluate information and compare information, ideas and opinions from different sources	B1: How information texts are organised B2: Understanding tables with words and symbols B3: Understanding tables with words and numbers C5: Understanding argument texts and identifying points of view	16 20 22 42	
Rt2.6 use organisational features and systems to locate texts and information	A1: Skimming, scanning and close reading A3: Finding main points and details B1: How information texts are organised B2: Understanding tables with words and symbols B3: Understanding tables with words and numbers E6: Paragraphs	4 10 16 20 22 70	B: page 32 E: page 56 F: page 64
Rt2.7 use different reading strategies to find and obtain information	A1: Skimming, scanning and close reading A3: Finding main points and details B1: How information texts are organised	4 10	A: page 24 B: page 32 C: page 40

Standard	Skills Book Section	Skills Book page	Teacher's Handbook Section and page
Rw: Vocabulary, word recognition and phonics			
Rw2.1 read and understand technical vocabulary	A2: Understanding difficult words	8	D: page 48
Rw2.2 use reference materials to find meanings of unfamiliar words	A2: Understanding difficult words	8	D: page 48
Ws: Grammar and Punctuation			
Ws1.1 write in complete sentences	E1: Sentences	60	
Ws1.2 use correct grammar	E2: Commas	62	
	E3: Apostrophes – the basics	64	
	E4: More on apostrophes	66	
	E5: Inverted commas	68	
	F2: Consistent use of tense	76	
	F3: Subject-verb agreement	78	
	F4: Using pronouns clearly	80	
Ws1.3 punctuate sentences correctly and use punctuation so that meaning is clear	E1: Sentences	60	
	E2: Commas	62	
Wt: Writing composition			
Wt2.1 plan and draft writing	E5: Paragraphs	70	D: page 48 E: page 56
Wt2.3 present ideas in logical/persuasive sequence; use paragraphs where appropriate	C3: Understanding explanation texts	34	A: page 24
	C4: Understanding persuasive texts	38	
	C5: Understanding argument texts and identifying points of view	42	
	E5: Paragraphs	70	
Wt2.4 use format and structure to organise writing for different purposes	C1: Identifying audience and purpose	26	B: page 32
	C2: Understanding descriptive texts	30	
	C3: Understanding explanation texts	34	
	C4: Understanding persuasive texts	38	
	C5: Understanding argument texts and identifying points of view	42	
	C6: Understanding formal and informal texts	46	
	E5: Paragraphs	70	
Wt2.5 use formal and informal language appropriate to purpose and audience	C6: Understanding formal and informal texts	46	

Standard	Skills Book Section	Skills Book page	Teacher's Handbook Section and page
Wt2.6 use different styles of writing for different purposes	C1: Identifying audience and purpose	26	A: page 24
	C2: Understanding descriptive texts	30	B: page 32
	C3: Understanding explanation texts	34	
	C4: Understanding persuasive texts	38	
	C5: Understanding argument texts and identifying points of view	42	
	C6: Understanding formal and informal texts	46	
Wt2.7 proof read and revise	D1: Spelling strategies		D: page 48
			E: page 56
Ws: Grammar and punctuation			
Ws2.1 construct complex sentences	E1: Sentences	60	F: page 64
	E2: Commas	62	
	F1: Using connectives	74	
	F2: Consistent use of tense	76	
Ws2.2 use correct grammar	E1: Sentences	60	F: page 64
	E2: Commas	62	
	E3: Apostrophes – the basics	64	
	E4: More on apostrophes	66	
	E5: Inverted commas	68	
	F2: Consistent use of tense	76	
	F3: Subject-verb agreement	78	
	F4: Using pronouns clearly	80	
Ws2.3 use pronouns so meaning is clear	F4: Using pronouns clearly	80	F: page 64
Ws2.4 punctuate sentences correctly	E1: Sentences	60	E: page 56
	E2: Commas	62	
	E3: Apostrophes – the basics	64	
	E4: More on apostrophes	66	
	E5: Inverted commas	68	
	F1: Using connectives	74	
Ww: Spelling and handwriting			
Ww2.1 spell correctly, including familiar technical words	D1: Spelling strategies	50	D: page 48
	D2: Plurals	52	
	D3: Words that sound the same	54	
	D4: Suffixes and double letters	56	

Standard	Skills Book Section	Skills Book page	Teacher's Handbook Section and page
SLlr: Listen and respond			
SLlr2.3 Respond to detailed or extended questions on a range of topics			A: page 24
SLc: Speak to communicate			
SLc2.1 Speak clearly and confidently in a way which suits the situation			D: page 48 E: page 56
SLc2.2 Make requests and ask questions to obtain detailed information in familiar and unfamiliar contexts			A: page 24
SLc2.3 Express clearly statements of fact, explanations, instructions, accounts, descriptions using appropriate structure, style and vocabulary			B: page 32 C: page 40 F: page 64
SLd: Engage in discussion			
SLd2.1 Make relevant contributions to help move discussions forward			B: page 32
SLd2.4 Support opinions and arguments with evidence			C: page 40

Mapping against Key Skills and GCSE

The charts below maps Adult Literacy Level 2 standards again the National Curriculum, Key Skills Communication and GCSE for speaking and listening, reading and writing.

Speaking and listening

National Curriculum Level 6	Adult Literacy Level 2	Key Skill - Level 2 C2.1 — Part A	Part B	GCSE
Pupils adapt their talk to the demands of different contexts with increasing confidence. Their talk engages the interests of the listener through the variety of its vocabulary and expression. Pupils take an active part in discussion, showing understanding of ideas and sensitivity to others. They are usually fluent in their use of standard English in formal situations.	**Listen and respond** to spoken language, including extended information and narratives, and follow detailed explanations and multi-step instructions of varying length, adapting response to speaker, medium and context. **Speak to communicate** straightforward and detailed information, ideas and opinions clearly, adapting speech and content to take account of the listeners(s), medium, purpose and situation. **Engage in discussion** with one or more people in a variety of different situations, making clear and effective contributions that produce outcomes appropriate to purpose and topic. In a wide range of formal and social exchanges: ▪ listen for and identify relevant information from extended explanations or presentations on a range of topics ▪ listen to, understand and follow lengthy or multi-step instructions and narratives on a range of topics and in a range of contexts ▪ speak clearly and confidently in a way that suits the situation ▪ respond to detailed or extended questions on a range of topics ▪ respond to criticism and criticise constructively ▪ make requests and ask questions to obtain detailed information in familiar and unfamiliar contexts ▪ express clearly statements of fact, explanations, instructions, accounts, descriptions, using appropriate structure, style and vocabulary ▪ present information and ideas in a logical sequence and provide further detail and development to clarify or confirm understanding ▪ make relevant contributions and help to move discussions forward ▪ adapt contributions to discussions to suit audience, context, purpose and situation ▪ use appropriate phrases for interruption and change of topic ▪ support opinions and arguments with evidence ▪ use strategies intended to reassure, e.g. body language and appropriate phraseology.	**Discuss:** use varied vocabulary and expressions to suit your purpose adapt what you say to suit different situations listen carefully to what others say identify the speakers intentions move the discussion forward. **Give a short talk:** prepare for the talk adapt your language to suit your subject, purpose and situation structure what you say to help listeners follow a line of thought or series of events use a variety of ways to support the main points of your talk including using images. **Part C Guidance:** **Discussion:** To present an argument, express ideas or opinions and exchange information judging effectively the amount to say and using a manner and tone of voice to suit the situation. To summarise, develop points and to focus on purpose. **Give short talk:** Avoiding or explaining technical terms and using a variety of techniques to engage the audience (e.g. keeping attention by varying tone of voice; giving examples; signalling new points; using images or other support to illustrate what you are saying).	**Take part in a group discussion:** 2.1a.1 make clear and relevant contributions in a way that suits your purpose and situation 2.1a.2 respond appropriately to others 2.1a.3 help to move the discussion forward. **Give a talk of at least 4 minutes:** 2.1b.1 speak clearly in a way that suits your subject, purpose and situation 2.1b.2 keep to the subject and structure your talk to help listeners follow what you are saying 2.1b.3 use appropriate ways to support your main points. **Use at least one image either to obtain information or to convey information in your discussion, your talk or one of the documents you write in order to help the audience/reader understand the points you are making.**	**A01** i. Communicate clearly and imaginatively, structuring and sustaining their talk and adapting it to different situations, using standard English appropriately; ii. Participate in discussion by both speaking and listening, judging the nature and purposes of contributions and the roles of participants; iii. Adopt roles and communicate with audiences using a range of techniques. The range assessed must include: explain, describe, narrate, explore, analyse, imagine, discuss, argue, persuade; in a variety of formal and informal contexts; and focus on extended individual contributions, group discussions and interaction, and drama-focused activities. **Grade C:** Candidates match their talk to the demands of different contexts. They use varied vocabulary and organise their talk to communicate clearly, engaging the interest of the listener. In discussion, candidates make significant contributions, varying how and when they participate. They show confident use of standard English in situations which require it.

Reading

National Curriculum Level 6	Adult Literacy Level 2	Key Skill – Level 2		GCSE
		Part A C2.1	**Part B**	

National Curriculum Level 6	Adult Literacy Level 2	Key Skill – Level 2 Part A / Part B	GCSE
In reading and discussing a range of texts, pupils identify different layers of meaning and comment on their significance and effect. They give personal responses to literary texts, referring to aspects of language, structure and themes in justifying their views. They summarise a range of information from different sources.	**Read and understand** a range of texts of varying complexity accurately and independently. **Read and obtain information** of varying length and detail from different sources. In a wide range of text types: ■ trace and understand the main events of continuous descriptive, explanatory and persuasive texts ■ identify the purpose of a text and infer meaning which is not explicit ■ identify the main points and specific detail ■ read an argument and identify the points of view ■ read critically to evaluate information and compare information, ideas and opinions from different sources ■ use organisational features and systems to locate texts and information ■ use different reading strategies to find and obtain information, e.g. skimming, scanning, detailed reading ■ summarise information from longer documents ■ read and understand technical vocabulary ■ use reference materials to find the meanings of unfamiliar words.	**Part A** **Read and summarise information:** ■ select and use different types of documents to obtain relevant information ■ skim documents to gain a general idea of content ■ scan documents to identify the information you need ■ recognise the writer's intentions ■ identify the main points, ideas and lines of reasoning from text and images ■ summarise information for a purpose. **Part B** **Read and summarise information from at least two documents about the same subject. Each document must be a minimum of 500 words long:** 2.2.1 select and read relevant documents 2.2.2 identify accurately the main points, ideas and lines of reasoning 2.2.3 summarise the information to suit your purpose. **Use at least one image either to obtain information or to convey information in your discussion, your talk or your write, in order to help the audience/reader understand the points you are making.** **Part C Guidance:** **Read and summarise information:** To obtain and compare facts, opinions and ideas, obtain instructions or directions from reports, text books and articles. To understand the writer's intention by tone, vocabulary and the structure of the text.	**A02** i. Read, with insight and engagement, making appropriate references to texts and developing and sustaining interpretations of them; ii. Distinguish between fact and opinion and evaluate how information is presented; iii. Follow an argument, identifying implications and recognising inconsistencies; iv. Select material appropriate to their purpose, collate material from different sources, and make cross references; v. Understand and evaluate how writers use linguistic, structural and presentational devices to achieve their effects, and comment on ways language varies and changes. The range of reading assessed includes: prose, poetry and drama; non-fiction texts; media texts. **Grade C:** Candidates show understanding of the ways in which meaning and information are conveyed in a range of literary and non-literary texts. They give personal and critical responses to literary texts, referring to aspects of language, structure and themes in justifying their views. They select and summarise a range of information from different sources.

Writing

National Curriculum Level 6	Adult Literacy Level 2	Key Skill - Level 2 C2.1 Part A	Part B	GCSE
Pupils' writing often engages and sustains the reader's interest, showing some adaptation of style and register to different forms, including using an impersonal style where appropriate. Pupils use a range of sentence structures and varied vocabulary to create effects. Spelling is generally accurate, including that of irregular words. Handwriting is neat and legible. A range of punctuation is usually used correctly to clarify meaning, and ideas are organised into paragraphs.	**Write to communicate** information, ideas and opinions clearly and effectively, using length, format and style appropriate to purpose, content and audience. In a wide range of documents: ■ Plan and draft writing ■ judge how much to write and the level of detail to include ■ present information and ideas in a logical or persuasive sequence, using paragraphs where appropriate ■ use format and structure to organise writing for different purposes ■ use formal and informal language appropriate to purpose and audience ■ use different styles of writing for different purposes, e.g. persuasive techniques, supporting evidence, technical vocabulary ■ construct complex sentences ■ use correct grammar, e.g. subject-verb agreement, correct and consistent use of tense ■ use pronouns so that their meaning is clear ■ punctuate sentences correctly and use punctuation accurately, e.g. commas, apostrophes, inverted commas ■ spell correctly words used most often in work, studies and daily life, including familiar technical words ■ proof-read and revise writing for accuracy and meaning ■ produce legible text.	**Write documents:** ■ use different formats for presenting information, including essays, reports and articles ■ structure your writing to help readers follow and understand your main points ■ use different styles of writing to suit different purposes ■ proof-read and where necessary redraft your documents so that: ■ spelling is accurate, including familiar technical words ■ sentences are formed correctly with accurate use of conjunctions ■ punctuation is accurate including use of commas, apostrophes and inverted commas.	**Write two different types of documents each one giving different information. One document must be at least 500 words long:** 2.3.1 present relevant information in a format that suits your purpose 2.3.2 use a structure and style of writing to suit your purpose 2.3.3 spell, punctuate and use grammar accurately 2.3.4 make your meaning clear. **Use at least one image either to obtain information or to convey information in your discussion, your talk or one of the documents you write, in order to help the audience/reader understand the points you are making.**	**AO3** i. Communicate clearly and imaginatively, using and adapting forms for different readers and purposes; ii. Organise ideas into sentences, paragraphs and whole texts using a variety of linguistic and structural features; iii. Use a range of sentence structures effectively with accurate punctuation and spelling. The range of writing assessed includes: explore, imagine, entertain; inform, explain, describe; argue, persuade, advise; analyse, review, comment; in a variety of forms and genres.
		Part C Guidance: **Write:** To produce documents such as letters, memos and extended essays or reports using paragraphs, headings and sub-headings to structure material.		**Grade C:** Candidates' writing engages and sustains the reader's interest. It shows adaptation of style and register to different forms, including using an impersonal style where appropriate. Candidates use a range of sentence structures and varied vocabulary to create effects. Paragraphing and correct punctuation are used to make the sequence of events or ideas coherent and clear to the reader. Spelling is accurate and handwriting is neat and legible.

Answers to Skill Book activities

Section A Reading for information and understanding

1 Skimming, scanning and close reading

1 a) **C** ☑ Cricket

b) left-arm

c) my role model and the best batsman in the world

d) Mohammad Kaif, Rahul Dravid

e) first match

2 a) **C** ☑ A newspaper article about the footballer Eniola Aluko

b) **B** ☑ Czech Republic

c) **D** ☑ law

d) **A** ☑ She thinks he's a great player.

e) **B** ☑ It's important to study because she will need a job if her football career ends early.

2 Understanding difficult words

1 b) **C** ☑ quickly

2 b) **A** ☑ oddly shaped

3 b) **C** ☑ make the skin less sensitive

4 b) **B** ☑ I will make sure you are happy with the finished job.

3 Finding main points and details

1 a) On attending at a fire, the firefighters have to make a quick assessment of the situation. As materials used in homes and factories change so does the way a fire is tackled. A house fire may require two appliances whereas a commercial or factory fire may involve several appliances as well as requiring thousands of litres of water and foam, plus the use of specialist equipment.

There is also the hazard of toxic fumes and heavy smoke which can be generated from the modern materials – for example foam-filled furniture. This makes tackling a fire that much more difficult and firefighters always go fully protected with equipment such as breathing apparatus as well as personal radio sets to keep them in contact with their colleagues at the scene, or back at brigade headquarters.

b) **A** ☑ When they arrive at a fire, firefighters need to work out quickly what equipment they need.

c) *Open question*

d) **C** ☑ How firefighters decide how to tackle a fire

e) **A** ☑ Toxic fumes

f) **D** ☑ Firefighting equipment

2 a) He has had a long and distinguished competition career, with many national and international titles to his credit.

b) **A** ☑ Early sporting interests

c) *Open question*

d) Captain

e) **D** ☑ Fighting moves you can use in karate

f) fast and effective   lightning-fast

g) **A** ☑ He joined the BKCC in 1970.

4 Test your skills

1 **A** ☑ To give general information about Rastafarianism

2 **C** ☑ Jamaica

3 **C** ☑ attractive

4 **B** ☑ What do Rastafarians believe?

5 **D** ☑ To worship God

6 **A** ☑ Rastafarians will return to their promised land after being slaves in Egypt and Babylon.

1 How information texts are organised

1 **B** Text type: email (From, To, Cc, Subject, informal greeting and sign-off)

C Text type: newspaper (headline, paragraphs, description of story)

D Text type: memo (Date, To, From, Subject, bullet points, request for something to be done)

E Text type: letter (address, date, Dear, Yours sincerely, writing to complain)

F Text type: report or essay (main heading, subheadings, bullet points, numbering, informative content)

2

Feature	Report	News article	Letter	Memo	E-mail
Main heading	✓	✓			
Subheading	✓				
Numbering	✓				
Bullet points	✓			✓	
Paragraphs	✓	✓	✓	✓	✓
Bold or italic text	✓			✓	
Persuasive language				✓	
Salutation			✓	✓	✓

3 a) (report)

b) The points need to be followed in that order.

c) The points do not need to be followed in any order.

d) **B** ☑ Because the writer wanted to make it easier to see what the different types of press-up are.

2 Understanding tables with words and symbols

1 a) ☑ Yes

b) No dogs.

c) Traethllyfn

d) Abermawr

e) Newport Sands

f) *Three of*: Poppit, Newport Sands, Cwm-yr-eglwys, Goodwick Sands, Abermawr, Abereiddy

g) It is accessible for disabled people.

h) Estuary, sand beach, rocky

i) **C** ☑ Cwm-yr-eglwys and Goodwick Sands

j) **D** ☑ In order to fit in more information

3 Understanding tables with words and numbers

1 a) Saturday

b) £25

c) £20

d) **D** ☑ £15

e) **C** ☑ by phone

f) **D** ☑ Men's long jump final

4 Test your skills

1 **B** ☑ A report about the advantages of taking exercise

2 **C** ☑ Types of exercise and calories they burn up in people of different weights

3 **D** ☑ They make important points stand out clearly.

4 **A** ☑ Skipping burns up more calories than any other exercise in the chart.

5 **C** ☑ People who weigh less burn up more calories than people who weigh more, when they do the same amount of exercise.

6 **C** ☑ Use italics to emphasise important words

1 Identifying audience and purpose

1 c) Explaining how to choose a primary school

Parents of young children

d) Persuading people to buy a new fragrance

General public

e) Persuading people to donate to famine relief

General public

f) Describing learning materials

Parents and children

2 b) To persuade women to buy a perfume

Women

c) To describe a scene in a place

General public, those interested in travelling

3 a) 16- to 25-year-olds, especially those feeling unmotivated

b) The Prince's Trust

c) **C** ☑ To persuade young people to take part in The Prince's Trust Team programme

d) The Team programme's free to join and you won't lose your benefit.

e) **D** ☑ During the programme, you will ... achieve nationally recognised qualifications

f) **B** ☑ During the programme, you will... have an amazing time

4 g) *For example*: What's stopping you from getting on with your life?

Tired, bored or broke? Not sure what to do? Don't know where to start? Then Team-up with The Prince's Trust

It's exciting It's challenging It's different It can help you get your life working

We offer exciting challenges, which help build your confidence and motivation, give you new skills and qualifications. Taking part will help you get the job you want.

f) **D** ☑ People are paid to take part in the Team programme

2 Understanding descriptive texts

1 a) *For example*: choking, scrambled, clutching, manhandled

b) **B** ☑ the lively bustling scene

c) **C** ☑ exciting and busy

d) layers of stinking fish

e) **D** ☑ It looked more like an exodus than a journey.

f) squawking chickens

g) **B** ☑ Detailed and descriptive

2 b) ☑ Fact

c) *For example*: They were really friendly on the phone and understood my nerves and my excitement.

d) **C** ☑ Factual and personal

e) *For example*: By showing her excitement at setting off on her journey, by comparing the exotic locations with her clock-watching temp job, by reassuring that the people at Travellers Worldwide understood her fears and were friendly.

f) I take a final look around my room

g) ☑ Both excited and frightened

h) **B** ☑ She wanted to travel to somewhere exotic and very different from Britain.

3 Understanding explanation texts

1 a) **C** ☑ To explain the process involved in tattooing

b) **D** ☑ People who want to understand how the process of tattooing works

c) **C** ☑ A diagram showing the process of creating a tattoo

d) *For example*: it would show visually what is being explained and described in the text.

2 subheading – Creating a tattoo: Outline, Shading and Colour

technical terms – flash

informative tone – *anywhere in main paragraphs*

use of bold text – *for example* flash; Outlining, or black work; Shading; Colour; Final cleaning and bandaging

process broken into series of steps – Outlining, or black work – Shading – Colour – Final cleaning and bandaging

words that show the order things happen in – start, After, then, Final, After

3 a) *Three of e.g.*: civil, libel, compensation, offender, victim

b) *anything from first two main paragraphs*

c) **A** ☑ The language is clear and simple to understand.

d) **A** ☑ To show where the pages link to other information

e) **C** ☑ ensure

f) **B** ☑ If you lose one you might get a criminal record.

g) **C** ☑ The difference between civil law and criminal law

h) **C** ☑ Clear and factual

4 Understanding persuasive texts

1 The services that help YOU care for your pets – Heading to emphasise main message

This year has been particularly difficult for us financially, and now we have a huge challenge / services on which so many pets and pet-owners depend – Words that appeal to the reader's feelings

please help us to continue with our good work – Request to the reader to do something

For the sake of animals like Blossom – Reason why the reader should do something

2 a) for unattached single travellers

b) Book a holiday with Union Holidays

c) *Two of:* GET AWAY Discover Book

d) **B** 100+ fabulous destinations

3 a) Children

b) To persuade people to go to the Amazatorium

c) funtabulous, excitabubbling, fizziwonderful

d) *For example:* To create a sense of fun and excitement

e) *Two of:* action-packed, thrill, adventure, amazing, wonderful, incredible, wonder, fun, excitement

f) Come to the funtabulous... *or* Enter the Amazatorium and let your dreams come true!

g) **D** ☑ Use of numbered points

h) **C** ☑ The incredible Amazatorium offers hands-on fun and excitement for everyone

i) **A** ☑ Exciting and persuasive

5 Understanding argument texts and identifying points of view

1 a) ☑ Argument

b) However, opponents of zoos claim that in practice zoos do little to help endangered animals. *Or* It is also claimed that animals raised in zoos are often mentally and physically unfit to cope with life in the wild. *Or* Opponents of zoos believe that zoo life is at best boring and unnatural for animals; at worst it can actually kill them, make them ill or drive them mad.

c) for animals on the endangered species list... zoos can be very positive

d) **C** ☑ Zoos protect 4000 different sorts of animals on the endangered species list

e) **B** ☑ Use of opinions

  C ☑ Use of facts

f) **A** ☑ Balanced and even-handed

g) Zoo life is at best boring and unnatural for animals. A C

There are around 4000 different types of animal on the endangered species list. B

Zoos can be very positive. A

Zoos are cruel and unnatural. A C

2 a) Persuasive ☑ It offers only one point of view.

b) It supports the view that smoking should not be banned in enclosed public places.

c) 68% of people reject a total ban on smoking in pubs, clubs and bars; 71% say proprietors should be allowed to choose their own policy on smoking.

d) **A** ☑ Such a move is neither popular nor appropriate.

e) **D** ☑ The writer believes that a ban on smoking in most public places would have bad effects on pubs and restaurants.

f) **C** ☑ Allowing everyone a free choice of whether they smoke and where they smoke.

6 Understanding formal and informal texts

1

Slang	I	Easy short words	I
Complex sentences	F	Short, simple sentences	I
No contractions	F	Passive verbs	F
Incomplete sentences	I	Contractions	I
Technical terms	F	Abbreviations	I

2

Slang	I	An e-mail inviting a friend to a party	I
A job application by e-mail	F	An e-mail inviting a friend of your grandmother's to a party	F
A job application by letter	F	A letter to the local newspaper	F
A text to your sister	I	A magazine article about fashion for teenagers	I
A memo giving important business information	F		

3 c) He was <u>eyeing</u> up the <u>talent</u> in the pub.

d) The date with him was <u>wicked</u>.

e) You're <u>sad</u> if you like reggae.

f) I <u>would be grateful</u> if you could send me more details. <u>Yours faithfully</u>, Jane.

g) I <u>am writing to confirm</u> my <u>resignation</u>.

h) He's really starting to <u>bug</u> me.

i) I'm <u>sick of</u> it all! <u>I quit!</u>

j) The <u>saline solution</u> <u>was added</u> to the liquid in the <u>test tube</u>.

k) <u>Please acknowledge receipt of</u> this letter.

4 (Just) to confirm I am (turning up) with my (mates) on 5th February for the (hen do). (There'll) be seven of us. (3) double rooms and a single (wd be cool). (We'll) want a table in the bar for a few (jars) before we go, but (won't) be staying at (yours) for dinner. (Hitting) the town instead!)
Cheers
Helen ☺

7 Test your skills

1 D ☑ To persuade the reader not to buy intensively farmed ducks

2 A ☑ Meat-eaters who are concerned about animal welfare

3 B ☑ The duck's diet affects the flavour of its meat.

4 B ☑ Ducks that dream of swimming on a pond

5 A ☑ To make the reader feel sorry for intensively farmed ducks

6 C ☑ Persuasive and informative

D Spelling words correctly

1 Spelling strategies

Words spelt correctly	Words spelt incorrectly – write the correct spelling!
usually	software
computer	knowledge
referred	viruses
annoying	currently
Promoting	businesses
	advertising
	emails

2 Plurals

1 A foxes   B benches   C wishes

D fizzes   E parties   F accessories

G diaries   H gameboys   I beliefs

J cliffs   K thieves   L tomatoes

M tattoos   N radios

2 A He's got two left foot/foots/(feet.)

B The (women)/wimen/wimmin were separated from the mans/(men)/mens.

C She came home with one chicken and two goose/gooses/(geese.)

D Who is going to look after the childs/childers/(children?)

3 ~~Brief lifes of the great inventors~~: Brief lives of the great inventors

~~Factorys in the Midlands~~: Factories in the Midlands

~~Ladys and Gentlemen: how to make an after-dinner speech~~: Ladies and Gentlemen: how to make an after-dinner speech

~~Nightmare Scenarioes – brushes with death in the jungle~~: Nightmare Scenarios – brushes with death in the jungle

~~Human Dynamoes~~: Human Dynamos

~~Thiefs and Swindlers~~: Thieves and Swindlers

3 Words that sound the same

1 A Would you like to put the shopping bags over <u>there</u>?

B Don't worry. <u>Their</u> parents will be here to pick them up soon.

C I think that <u>they're</u> a lovely couple.

D <u>There</u> are boy bands better than that.

E I'm sure that <u>they're</u> coming.

F I think that I can hear <u>their</u> car pulling up outside.

2 A If you're (too)/to/two nervous, you won't perform your best.

B Jake wanted to go too/to/two both gigs.

C Too/To/(Two's) company, but three's a crowd.

D Use the bridge too/(to)/two cross the rail track.

E Her intention was too/(to)/two break the school record.

3 We <u>are</u> going on holiday with <u>our</u> friends tomorrow. <u>Our</u> bus leaves at 10 a.m. and we <u>are</u> pretty certain we'll get to <u>our</u> hotel by <u>our</u> planned time of 8 p.m. <u>Are</u> you sure that you don't want to join <u>our</u> party?

4 *Open question*.

5 I know you <u>were</u> going to come shopping with me, but I've gone on my own. I don't want to go <u>where</u> we usually go, and I don't want you telling me what to <u>wear</u>. To be honest I don't know <u>where</u> our relationship is going: <u>we're</u> not seeing eye to eye at the moment, are we? It <u>wears</u> me out just thinking about it.

4 Suffixes and double letters

1 flagging flagged

2 gossiping gossiped

3 beading beaded

4 inspired inspiring inspiration

5 ~~carveing~~: carving

~~mooreings~~: moorings

~~sking~~: skiing

~~possibley~~: possibly

~~sunbatheing~~: sunbathing

~~bikeing~~: biking

~~stuning~~: stunning

~~exhilarateing~~: exhilarating

~~siping~~: sipping

~~seting~~: setting

5 Test your skills

1 C ☑ unfortunately

2 D ☑ they're

3 B ☑ allowed

4 D ☑ whether

5 B ☑ until

6 B ☑ businesses

7 C ☑ sincerely

8 C ☑ affects

E Using punctuation correctly

1 Sentences

1 b) How many times have I asked you not to do that?

c) You should have seen him blush!

d) Go to your room at once!

e) It all began one dark and stormy night.

2 a) D ☑ They are not a complete sentence.

b) A ☑ line 4

c) C ☑ line 9

d) C ☑ line 8

e) D ☑ line 7

f) *For example*: Don't let your house get stuck in the past! Then call Stokes today! You have nothing to lose and everything to gain!

2 Commas

1 a) ourselves, C

kids, A

Centre, B

Tesco's, B

peace, A

only, C

b) treadmills, rowing machines, weights

   courts, so

   pool, 25 metres long, is accompanied

2 a) It is important that children learn how to control their own behaviour as they get older. Parents are important role models for their children in helping them to learn how to do this.

   b) Every parent experiences frustration with his or her child at various times. A parent will often feel tempted to smack in the heat of the moment.

   c) Needless to say,

   d) Parents who continue to smack their children, may simply not know about other methods that work.

3 Apostrophes

1 everything's – everything is

   I've – I have

   I'm – I am

   How's – How is

   I'll – I will

   wouldn't – would not

   I've – I have

2 a) **B** ☑ Cheryl's café

   b) **A** ☑ Today's £4 specials

   c) **B** ☑ Fish and chips with mushy peas

   d) **D** ☑ Don't delay – come in today!

   e) **C** ☑ Your fish is our command!

4 More on apostrophes

1 It's the law

   GENTLEMEN'S CLOAKROOM

   JAMES' ROOM *or* JAMES'S ROOM

2 **The Rhythm Crew and MC Robbys** [[X] Robby's] **regular under-eighteen's** [[X] under-eighteens'] **night.** Its [[X] It's] for you if you're into full on R&B, Grime & Hip Hop Vibe's [[X] Vibes], Open Mic battles and Dance Comps.

Live on stage – **Random Less.** Following on from their hugely successful video debut and live appearances, **Random Less** [[X] Less' *or* Less's] music will bring it back with a bang, live and direct on Bliss' [[☑]] stage. Blisses' [[X] Bliss'] tradition of showcasing huge UK artists [[X] artists'] music, such as Dizzie Rascal & Kano, continues with yet another gig that will lift the roof.

Who'se [[X] Who's] goin' to be there?

childrens [[X] children's] theatre

3 It's a cold night and the moon is out, its shape clear through the trees. The old house stands empty and silent. Part of its roof is lying on the ground and part is hanging off as though it's about to fall at any moment. It's a weird old place. Its rafters are sound, its brickwork is secure, yet it's creepy.

5 Inverted commas

1 'American Beauty' – [2]

   'Fight Club' – [2]

   'down-to-earth' – [3]

   'mope' – [3]

   'Creepy, funny, poignant, and stunningly imaginative' – [1]

2 a) They are in inverted commas.

   b) 'If only you'd got a move on, this would never have happened.'

   c) 'So, what do we do now?' Nadine asked.

   d) ☑ No

   e) 'Well, you think of something, then,' Kofi grunted.

   f) The words are not direct speech.

6 Paragraphs

1 a) It starts a new topic.

   b) good exercise and healthy eating. // I note that you have not yet developing a personal programme. // I hope that you enjoy your membership

2 a) Sultan of Oman. // Ranulph has been an explorer

      longest journey in south polar history. // In 2000 Ranulph tried

      in his garden shed. // Four months after

in Singapore, Asia. // Ranulph's expeditions have

b) On his own __Number 3__

Early life __Number 1__

Charitable endeavour __Number 5__

Explorer and adventurer __Number 2__

Marathon man __Number 4__

7 Test your skills

1 **C** ☑ Take out the full stop and change 'And' to 'and'.

2 **B** ☑ A full stop after 'yesterday'.

3 **A** ☑ mark off the words from the rest of the sentence

4 **C** ☑ 3, 6 and 7

5 **C** ☑ line 6

6 **D** ☑ line 7

7 **B** ☑ lines 4 and 5

8 **D** ☑ line 11

F Using good grammar

1 Using connectives

1 **A** She snacked too much after school, __so__ she's not hungry now.

   B __Because__ he arrived late, the manager gave him a verbal warning.

   C __After__ you left, I read until midnight.

   D Kieran studied at weekends, __in order to__ get a good degree.

   E He went out for a walk, __although__ it was still raining.

2 b) We'll need to leave on time so we can be sure we'll get there on time.

   c) He'll need to save £5 a week because he wants to buy the bike himself.

   d) He sent a pass down the touchline, although Beckham was there to intercept it.

3 a) Some people would say celebrities are people who are famous for doing nothing, __but__ is this fair?

   __Although__ some celebrities, such as many actors, musicians and sportspeople, are genuinely talented

Many people say they only buy the magazines __and__ watch the shows in order to laugh, __but__ secretly they really enjoy keeping tabs on what their favourite celebrities are doing.

b) **A** ☑ because

c) **B** ☑ Because of

d) **C** ☑ so

2 Consistent use of tense

1 At Drayfield Manor School a peer anti-bullying group was set up last year to support pupils who (were)/are/will be experiencing bullying. In January the Year 12 tutor (asked)/asks/will ask for six volunteers to lead the group. They then (worked)/work/will work with representatives from each year group to look at the results of a bullying survey that had been sent to all pupils.

Last March the representatives (were)/are/will be given training on how to support other pupils who are experiencing bullying. This training (was)/is/will be highly successful. A qualified counsellor from the organisation 'Stamp out Bullying' (taught)/teaches/will teach our pupils about how to support their peers.

Now anyone from Year 7-11 who was/(is)/will be experiencing bullying found/(can find)/will find the pupil counsellors each day at lunchtime and after school.

2 a) **B** ☑ the present

   b) **A** ☑ the past

   c) **A** ☑ have and go

   d) **C** ☑ told and went

3 Subject-verb agreement

1 We are seeking an experience Fitter who
   ~~works~~
   <u>work</u> locally and can move between our
                                        have
   two garages in North London. You <u>has</u> a

   minimum of 3–4 years experience within a

   Bodyshop and must have your own tools. You
   are
   <u>is</u> a good communicator, self-motivated and

   able to meet targets and deadlines.

You will work in a friendly team with other
Fitters, and the job ~~are~~ [is] replacing damaged
bodywork and stripping and fitting door
panels, wheel arches, bumpers and trims. If
you ~~is~~ [are] looking for a fantastic opportunity
to progress in a fast expanding company
and ~~has~~ [have] the experience and skills required,
contact us now.

2 a) They goes to the cinema every Thursday. ☒

   Katherine does make an effort to phone
   regularly. ☑

   b) Either my brother or my cousin are going
   to the match with you. ☒

   Nobody really wants to stay that late. ☑

   c) Federer and Roddick are the best tennis
   players on the circuit. ☑

   Hannah and two of her friends has gone
   away for the weekend. ☒

   d) Teachers' skills in developing their pupils'
   creativity varies from school to school. ☒

   The attendance level in all our courses has
   risen hugely. ☑

3 a) Abdul and Karim <u>are</u> going to the match.

   b) Every packet of crisps <u>has</u> been eaten.

   c) Everybody <u>is</u> going clubbing.

   d) My complaint about the deliveries <u>is</u> being
   ignored.

4 Using pronouns clearly

1 b) You should put the (baby) to bed before *he*
   gets tired. ☑

   You should put the baby to bed before
   they get tired. ☒

   c) (Students) should bring an example from
   their own experience. ☑

   Students should bring an example from
   your own experience. ☒

   d) As soon as Dave opened the door, *you* could
   see that there had been a break-in. ☒

   As soon as (Dave) opened the door, *he* could
   see that there had been a break-in. ☑

e) Mina asked (Neelam) and (Navid) if *they* could
   help her. ☑

   Mina asked Neelam and Navid if *she* could
   help her. ☒

2 a) Gina could hardly believe how many
   people turned to look at (Gina) <u>her</u>

   b) The tree was creaking loudly, as it (the tree)
   was about to fall down. <u>it</u>

   c) Chloe and Sam went to a party where
   (Chloe and Sam) had a great time. <u>they</u>

3 (They offer:) It offers
   (we:) they
   (This is:) These are
   (We go:) They go
   (she:) they

5 Test your skills

1 **C** ☑ lines 6, 9, 12 and 21
2 **D** ☑ because
3 **B** ☑ decorated
4 **C** ☑ work
5 **B** ☑ their
6 **D** ☑ although
7 **B** ☑ will be

21

Whole class progress tracking grid

Use the chart below to track when each of your students has complete a section in the Skills Book and what their score is in the end of section test.

Student Name	A Reading for information and understanding		B Understanding the features of different texts		C Understanding how writers achieve their purpose		D Spelling words correctly		E Punctuation		F Grammar		G Preparing for the test	
	Completed	End of test score	Completed	End of test score	Completed	End of test score	Completed	End of test score	Completed	End of test score	Completed	End of test score	Completed	End of test score

Certificate

Awarded to

For successfully completing a course in

Adult Literacy Level 2

Date: ....

Signed: ....

A Reading for information and understanding

(pages 4–15 in the Skills Book)

Speaking and Listening	Reading	Writing
SLlr/2.3 Respond to detailed or extended questions on a range of topics.	**Rt/2.3** Identify main points and specific detail.	**Wt/2.3** Present ideas in logical / persuasive sequence; use paragraphs where appropriate.
SLc/2.2 Make requests and ask questions to obtain information.	**Rt/2.7** Use different reading strategies to find and obtain information.	**Wt/2.6** Use different styles of writing for different purposes.

The list indicated above involves the standards covered in the Skills Book and the standards covered in what follows.

Section outline

Section A covers a range of reading skills that will be assessed in the Adult Literacy test. Poor readers will need a great deal of support to learn these skills. Good readers will already use many of these skills intuitively but will find that their test performances improve once they understand the skills more explicitly.

The reading skills are organised in the following sections:

■ skimming, scanning, and close reading

■ understanding difficult words

■ finding main points and details.

Approaches to teaching

You will need to teach two important concepts in this section:

■ there are different reading skills, which are used for different purposes

■ if students actively engage with texts, rather than read passively, they will understand a great deal more.

Encourage students to decide which reading skill they need to use to answer a particular question in the test. This will save them time. For example, a question may best be answered by skimming or scanning the text, and close reading may not be necessary.

Whole class tip

Approach some of the tests in this book as whole class activities and encourage the pupils to identify the reading skill or skills that each question is testing.

It is important to teach the students how to read a text **actively**. Encourage students to become used to reading texts with a pen, and annotate the text while they are reading. This will help them **engage** with the text, rather than just passively read it.

As the students become more confident readers they should be able to annotate:

■ **words or phrases** that might answer the test questions

■ **words** they do not know, which may need thought when answering questions

■ **topic sentences** that define the subject of a paragraph and help to identify the main points of a text

■ **connectives**, i.e. words or phrases that link ideas together, such as *however*, *secondly*, *in addition*. Identifying connectives helps students to see the relationship between ideas in a text.

When preparing students for the test, teach them to read the questions before they start to read the text. This will mean their reading has a purpose – to answer specific questions. It is easier to read a text if you know why you are reading it.

The most important thing you can do is to model reading skills with students. You can do this with individuals or with the whole class, using an OHP or digital projector.

■ Choose one of the tests and talk about your thought processes as you read it.

■ Explain how you skim and scan, and how the two skills are different.

■ Explain how you make sense of difficult words.

■ Above all, show that you sometimes have problems answering questions but that you can engage with the text in order to work things out.

Linked Speaking and Listening and Writing activities

This unit will give you the opportunity to target relevant Speaking and Listening and Writing standards, using activities such as the following.

Speaking and Listening

■ *Paired work:* one person is an interviewer and the other is a famous sportsperson. The interviewer asks about the sportsperson's life and career *(SLlr/2.3; SLc/2.2)*.

■ *Group work:* you are a group of sports journalists. Agree a list of the top five sportspeople of the year and your reasons for including each one *(SLlr/2.3; SLc/2.2)*.

Writing

■ Imagine that you are Monty Panesar or Eniola Aloku. Write a newspaper article about the pressures you face as a prominent player in your chosen sport *(Wt/2.3; Wt/2.6)*.

■ Write an imaginary interview with a famous sportsperson of your choice *(Wt/2.3; Wt/2.6)*.

Photocopiable worksheets

The following photocopiable sheets are included in Section A:

A1 Different text types

A2 Text types and expected features

A3 Use different reading skills to obtain information 1

A4 Use different reading skills to obtain information 2

A5 Use different reading skills to obtain information 3

A6 Understanding difficult words.

A1 Different text types

This worksheet accompanies **pages 16–17** in the *Level 2 Skills Book*

Name _____ Date _____

Here are three different texts. Choose the sort of text you think each one is, from the following list, and write the letter below:

- ■ **A** newspaper article
- ■ **C** formal letter
- ■ **E** persuasive essay
- ■ **G** advertisement.
- ■ **B** memo
- ■ **D** e-mail
- ■ **F** informal letter

Afterwards, annotate each text to highlight the conventions used that helped you to identify its text type.

Hi Esther. Can you send me the following urgently: Jimi Hendrix, Electric Ladyland, 1 copy; 3 Doors Down, Away From the Sun, 3 copies; the new Razorlight album, 6 copies. Hope your holiday went well.	line 1 / line 2 / line 3
Best wishes, Sue.	line 4
Sue. Received your order today. I've got almost everything in stock and will post stuff today. The only CD we don't have is the new Razorlight and I will forward that asap. Thanks for your continued support.	line 5 / line 6 / line 7
E xx	line 8

1 Text type _____

14 Sherborne Road — line 1
Yeovil — line 2
Somerset — line 3
BA10 6SQ — line 4

Tuesday 28th July 2006 — line 5

The Manager — line 6
Letts' Bank — line 7
Yeovil — line 8
Somerset — line 9
BA2 4TW — line 10

Dear Sir — line 11

I have had some recent financial difficulties and seek your help. I would be extremely grateful if you would allow me to increase my overdraft facility by £300 until October. — line 12 / line 13 / line 14 / line 15

Yours faithfully, — line 16

Andy Borrell — line 17

Andy Borrell — line 18

2 Text type _____

Nurse Celebrates by Getting Plastered — line 1 / line 2

Yesterday, Sue Hayward, an attractive blonde 28-year-old nurse at Staffordshire General Hospital, celebrated winning a massive jackpot of £35,000. She threw a riotous party for all the nurses, doctors and patients on E4, the ward she has worked on for three years. David Blakey, 64, a patient on the ward said, "She's an angel. I haven't enjoyed myself so much in hospital for ages." Nurse Hayward plans to buy herself a new car and then take all of her family on a well-deserved holiday. — line 3 / line 4 / line 5 / line 6 / line 7 / line 8 / line 9 / line 10 / line 11 / line 12 / line 13 / line 14 / line 15 / line 16 / line 17

3 Text type _____

Text types and expected features

This worksheet accompanies **pages 16–17** in the *Level 2 Skills Book*

Name _____   Date _____

Table 1 contains a range of text types. Fill in the table by ticking the features you would expect in each text type. To help you, refer to Table 2, which explains what effect can be achieved by each feature.

Text types	Heading	Subheadings	Numbering	Bullet points	Paragraphs	Bold or italic text
Formal letter accepting an invitation						
Memo explaining procedure						
Email to a friend						
Newspaper article						
Information leaflet						
Advertisement in a magazine						

Table 1 A range of text types and expected features

Features	What can be achieved by each feature
Headings	tell the reader what the text is about.
Subheadings	tell the reader what the subject of a section is. They can also be used to break up a long text into smaller sections.
Numbering	tells the reader that the points have been placed in a specific order.
Bullet points	tell the reader that there is a list of different points, but they might have been placed in any order.
Paragraphs	organise the text and keep points on a similar subject all together.
Bold or italic text	highlights important words or phrases.

Table 2 Features and what each can achieve

Use different reading skills to obtain information 1

This worksheet accompanies **pages 4–7** in the *Level 2 Skills Book*

Name _____   Date _____

You know there are different reading skills:

■ skimming;   ■ scanning;   ■ close reading.

You use these different reading skills for different purposes.

Look at the following definitions. Draw lines to join the definitions to the correct reading skills.

Skimming		means reading a text carefully so you can really understand it.
Scanning		means looking over a text quickly to find out what it's about.
Close reading		means quickly running your eyes across the page to find the answer to a particular question.

In the table below, say whether you would use **skimming**, **scanning** or **close reading** for each of the tasks listed. Then write why you would use that reading skill. The first one has been done for you.

	Task	Reading skill
1	To find the date when something happened.	*scanning, because I'm only looking for a date – I don't need to close read.*
2	To get a general impression of what the passage is about.	
3	To locate a subheading.	
4	To find the name of someone who has done a particular thing.	
5	To work out what a graph tells you.	
6	To work out the author's attitude towards something.	

A4 Use different reading skills to obtain information 2

This worksheet accompanies **pages 4–7** in the *Level 2 Skills Book*

Name _____   Date _____

Before you read the passage at the bottom of the page, read
the questions and circle the reading skill that you would use to
answer each type of question. The first one has been done for you.

1 Who is this article mainly about?

    A ☐ (skimming) **B** ☐ scanning **C** ☐ close reading

2 Will this passage tell you the name of Sebastian Coe's main
rival in the 1980s?

    A ☐ skimming **B** ☐ scanning **C** ☐ close reading

3 In which year did Sebastian Coe win an Olympic gold medal
for the 1500 m?

    A ☐ skimming **B** ☐ scanning **C** ☐ close reading

4 In which year will the Summer Olympics be held in London?

    A ☐ skimming **B** ☐ scanning **C** ☐ close reading

5 What would be a good title for this article?

    A ☐ skimming **B** ☐ scanning **C** ☐ close reading

6 What qualities does Sebastian Coe have that make him well
suited to his job?

    A ☐ skimming **B** ☐ scanning **C** ☐ close reading

Sebastian Coe, who headed the team that brought the 2012   line 1
Summer Olympics to London, is well qualified for the job.   line 2
He has set eight world records and won four Olympic medals   line 3
in middle distance running. Coe also studied economics at   line 4
Loughborough University.   line 5

Through the late 1970s and early 1980s Sebastian Coe, and   line 6
his British rival Steve Ovett, dominated 800 m and 1500 m   line 7
running. The height of their rivalry was the 1980 Olympic   line 8
Games, where Ovett won the 800 m and Coe won the 1500 m.   line 9

Now retired from running, Sebastian Coe has an opportunity   line 10
to put something back into athletics. He is chairperson of   line 11
the London Organising Committee of the Olympic Games. It   line 12
is this committee that has to ensure that the 2012 Olympic   line 13
Games in London are a success.   line 14

A5 # Use different reading skills to obtain information 3

This worksheet accompanies **pages 4–7** in the *Level 2 Skills Book*

Name _____   Date _____

Read these questions, then read the passage below and answer them.

1 Who is this article mostly about?

A ☐ Steve Ovett   **B** ☐ Steve Cram

C ☐ Sebastian Coe

2 Who was Sebastian Coe's main rival in the 1980s?

A ☐ Steve Ovett   **B** ☐ Steve Cram

C ☐ Said Aouita

3 In which year did Sebastian Coe win an Olympic gold medal for the 1500 m?

A ☐ 1976   **B** ☐ 1980   **C** ☐ 1986

4 In which year will the Summer Olympics be held in London?

A ☐ 2021   **B** ☐ 2020   **C** ☐ 2012

5 What would be a good title for this article?

A ☐ The Olympic Games

B ☐ The 2012 London Olympic Games

C ☐ Sebastian Coe returns to the Olympics

6 What qualities does Sebastian Coe have that make him well suited to his job?

A ☐ His athletics experience and his economics degree

B ☐ His rivalry with Steve Ovett and his ability to chair meetings

C ☐ He lives in London and he can run fast

> Sebastian Coe, who headed the team that brought the 2012 Summer   line 1
> Olympics to London, is well qualified for the job. He has set eight   line 2
> world records and won four Olympic medals in middle distance   line 3
> running. Coe also studied economics at Loughborough University.   line 4
>
> Through the late 1970s and early 1980s Sebastian Coe, and his British   line 5
> rival Steve Ovett, dominated 800 m and 1500 m running. The height of   line 6
> their rivalry was the 1980 Olympic Games, where Ovett won the 800 m   line 7
> and Coe won the 1500 m.   line 8
>
> Now retired from running, Sebastian Coe has an opportunity to put   line 9
> something back into athletics. He is chairperson of the London   line 10
> Organising Committee of the Olympic Games. It is this committee that   line 11
> has to ensure that the 2012 Olympic Games in London are a success.   line 12

A6 Understanding difficult words

This worksheet accompanies **pages 8–9** in the *Level 2 Skills Book*

Name _____ Date _____

When you are reading you will sometimes come across words that you do not understand. However, with a little thought you can often work out the meaning of a word you do not know.

Read this passage about Kelly Holmes. Some words have been underlined. In the table below circle another word with the same meaning for each of the underlined words. The first one has been done for you.

Kelly Holmes	line 1
Kelly Holmes had some success as a junior athlete, winning the English Schools' 1500 m title at both junior and senior levels. At the age of 18 she joined the army and for the next four years her military career became more _significant_ to her than her athletics career.	line 2 line 3 line 4 line 5
However, while she was in the army Kelly Holmes realised that she could run much more _swiftly_ than many of the women who were representing England. Consequently, in 1992 she returned to athletics and has since had _phenomenal_ success. For example, in 1995 she set British records at 800 m and 1500 m and obtained a bronze medal in the World Championships. Like all top athletes, Kelly Holmes has suffered from injuries in her career, but these injuries have not stopped her _advancement_. In the 2000 Olympic Games she won silver and bronze medals, but her greatest _accomplishment_ was the two gold medals she was awarded in the 2004 Olympic Games, after winning both the 800 m and the 1500 m.	line 6 line 7 line 8 line 9 line 10 line 11 line 12 line 13 line 14 line 15 line 16
In _acknowledgement_ of Kelly Holmes's achievements, particularly in the 2004 Olympic Games, she was made a Dame in the 2004 New Year's Honours List.	line 17 line 18 line 19

Original word from the passage	Circle the word with the same meaning
significant	(important) time-consuming, large
swiftly	bird-like, quickly, immediately
phenomenal	disappointing, average, extraordinary
advancement	progress, expansion, getting older
accomplishment	skill, achievement, difficulty
acknowledgement	agreement, knowledge, tribute

B Understanding the features of different texts

(pages 16–25 in the Skills Book)

Speaking and Listening	Reading	Writing
SLc/2.3 Express clearly statements of fact, explanations, instructions, accounts, descriptions using appropriate structure, style and vocabulary. **SLd/2.1** Make relevant contributions to help move discussions forward.	**Rt/2.2** Identify purpose of a text and infer meaning which is not explicit. **Rt/2.6** Use organisational features and systems to locate texts and information. **Rt/2.7** Use different reading strategies to find and obtain information.	**Wt/2.4** Use format and structure to organise writing for different purposes. **Wt/2.6** Use different styles of writing for different purposes.

The list indicated above includes the standards covered in the Skills Book and the standards covered in what follows.

Section outline

Section B covers a range of reading skills that will be assessed in the Adult Literacy test. Poor readers will need a great deal of support to develop these skills. Good readers will already use many of these skills intuitively but will find that their test performances improve once they understand the skills more explicitly.

The reading skills are organised in the following sections:

- how information texts are organised
- understanding tables with words and symbols
- understanding tables with words and numbers.

Approaches to teaching

This section covers two different skill areas.

1 Organisation of information texts:
- how to respond to language features of different texts
- how to respond to presentational features of different texts.

2 Understanding tables:
- deciding what you need to find out
- reading the separate features in a table.

Organisation of information texts

Students need to understand the conventional language features and presentational features associated with different text types. The table on sheet B6 summarises a range of language and presentational features that are often found in four common text types. With knowledge of these conventional language and presentational features, students can explore a range of text types and their purposes. Writers will use language and presentational features deliberately for effect. These features collectively influence the message of the text.

Whole class tip

Give the students a range of text types and ask them to annotate the texts in order to identify the language and presentational features. Afterwards, encourage the students to think about what effect each of these features has.

When you study different texts ask the students questions, such as:

- What effect do the colours of the advertisement have?
- Why has the writer used so many adjectives and adverbs?
- Do the bullet points help to structure the information?
- In what way does the caption define the content of the photograph?

Reading tables

Students are faced with three key problems when they have to read tables:

1 There is so much abstract text, weak students are overwhelmed and give in.

2 Information can be presented in a deliberately misleading way.

3 The students are not actually sure which information they need to answer a question.

Encourage students to approach a table in the following way:

- read the title above the table to find out what the table represents

- read the label underneath the table to find out what the table represents

- read the titles given to all rows and all columns

- read any footnotes that are provided

- find out what any symbols represent.

Whole class tip

Model to the class how you read tables. Articulate how you read all of the features. When you look for a piece of information define clearly what you have to look for and then show how you use one finger to trace across a row and how you use another finger to trace down a column.

Linked Writing and Speaking and Listening activities

This unit will give you the opportunity to target relevant Speaking and Listening and Writing standards, using activities such as the following.

Writing

- Refer to the table on page 20 of the Skills Book. Ask the students to write a short piece of organised prose for a leaflet advertising Pembrokeshire as a holiday resort. They should write one paragraph about Lower Fishguard and another about Aberfelin. The following connectives may be helpful: *in addition, also, moreover, furthermore, however, unfortunately. (Wt/2.4)*

- Using the information from the table on page 20 of the Skills Book, ask the students to write one paragraph about a Pembrokeshire holiday resort suitable for retired people, and one paragraph about a Pembrokeshire holiday resort more suitable for teenagers. The selection of relevant material is important and they should also write in styles appropriate for their audiences. *(Wt/2.6)*

- Provide the students with a piece of text that presents a great deal of information, e.g. a piece of writing from a science textbook, with any tables or illustrations omitted. Ask the students to work in groups to present the information in a table. *(Wt/2.4)*

Speaking and Listening

Students working in groups to find information from a table will learn from each other's strategies. These speaking and listening activities will facilitate this collaborative learning.

- Provide the students with a table, or tables on the same theme, from a geography textbook. Ask the students to study the tables, interpret any ambiguities present, and to digest the information. Their next task is to work together to present the information orally to the rest of the class. *(SLc/2.3)*

Photocopiable worksheets

The following photocopiable sheets are included in Section B:

B1 Languages features and presentational features 1

B2 Language features and presentational features 2

B3 Reading tables effectively 1

B4 Reading tables effectively 2

B5 Reading tables effectively 3

B6 Conventional language features and presentational features

B1 Language features and presentational features

This worksheet accompanies **pages 16–20** in the *Level 2 Skills Book*

Name _____   Date _____

In different text types we expect to see:

■ different language features

■ different presentational features.

Fill in the table below. The table records the different language features and presentational features found in different text types. Some of the answers have been filled in for you.

Text type	Example	Language features	Presentational features
Information leaflet	Health leaflet warning about the dangers of smoking	* Written in the third person (e.g. he, she, it) * Formal language * Technical language * Simple sentences * Carefully structured	
Advertisement	Advertisement to sell a soft drink		* Bright colours * Eye-catching illustrations * Possibly cartoon characters
Newspaper report	Report on national disaster	* Written in the third person * Formal language * Range of sentence structures * Emotive language, with extensive use of adjectives and adverbs * Carefully structured	
Letter	Letter to travel agent to complain about disastrous holiday		* Address * Salutation (e.g. Dear Sir.) * Paragraphs

B2 Language features and presentational features

This worksheet accompanies **pages 16–20** in the *Level 2 Skills Book*

Name _____ Date _____

Use your knowledge and your reading experience to fill in the following table. The table records different language features and different presentational features that we might expect in different text types. Choose the answers from the boxes under the table. You will need to use some of the boxes more than once.

Text type	Example	Language features	Presentational features
Front cover of magazine	Teenage magazine aimed at boys		
Home page of a website	Website advertising holidays for retired people		
Page from a textbook	A science textbook aimed at KS4 pupils		

Informal language

Slang

Aimed directly at target audience

Formal language

Third person

Bright colours

Formal colours

Black and white

Range of informal fonts

Range of formal fonts

Cartoons

Diagrams

Photographs

Technical language

Eye-catching illustrations / photographs

Hyperlinks

B3 Reading tables effectively 1

This worksheet accompanies **pages 20–23** in the *Level 2 Skills Book*

Name _____   Date _____

Look at the following table and then answer the questions.

Country	Population[1]	Birth rate[2]	Death rate[3]	Infant mortality[4]	Life expectancy[5]
Australia	131	12.14	7.51	4.63	80.50
Brazil	188	16.56	6.17	28.6	71.97
China	1314	13.25	6.97	23.12	72.58
France	61	11.99	9.14	3.24	79.73
Germany	82	8.25	10.62	4.12	78.80
India	1095	22.01	8.18	54.63	64.71
Japan	127	9.37	9.16	3.24	81.25
UK	61	10.71	10.13	5.08	78.54
USA	298	14.14	8.26	6.43	77.85

Figures based on CIA World Book (2006)

Footnotes
[1] Population in millions.
[2] Births per 1000 population.
[3] Deaths per 1000 population.
[4] Deaths per 1000 live births.
[5] From birth.

1 How are the countries in this table organised?

A ☐ In order of population size

B ☐ Randomly

C ☐ In rank order of life expectancy

D ☐ In alphabetical order

2 What is the population of China?

A ☐ 1314   **B** ☐ 1314 million

B ☐ 1,314,000   **D** ☐ 1314 billion

3 Which of the following statements is **not** true, according to the chart?

A ☐ Japan has a larger population than Germany.

B ☐ The birth rate of every country is higher than its death rate.

C ☐ Life expectancy in the UK is higher than in the USA.

D ☐ Infant mortality is higher in the UK than in France.

4 Which country has the highest death rate?

A ☐ UK   **B** ☐ Japan

C ☐ France   **D** ☐ Germany

5 According to this table, which two countries seem to be the best places to have babies?

A ☐ France and Japan   **B** ☐ China and India

C ☐ UK and USA   **D** ☐ Germany and Brazil

B4 Reading tables effectively 2

This worksheet accompanies **pages 20–23** in the *Level 2 Skills Book*

Name _____   Date _____

Look at the following table and then answer the questions.

Average daily sales of most popular UK daily newspapers

Average Daily sales

1	Daily Mail
2	Daily Record
3	Daily Star
4	Daily Express
5	Financial Times
6	The Guardian
7	The Independent
8	Daily Mirror
9	The Sun
10	The Daily Telegraph
11	The Times

Footnotes
1 *Figures rounded to nearest 1000.*
2 *Figures relate to average daily circulation figures November 2005.*

1   From this table, what are the average daily sales of *The Times*?

   A ☐ 500 000   **B** ☐ 1 000 000   **C** ☐ 750 000

2   What can you say about the daily sales of the *Daily Express* and the *Daily Mirror*?

   A ☐ They sell about the same number of copies each day

   B ☐ The *Daily Mirror* sells about twice as many copies as the *Daily Express*

   C ☐ The *Daily Express* sells about twice as many copies as the *Daily Mirror*

3   Which daily newspaper has the most sales?

   A ☐ *The Daily Telegraph*

   B ☐ The *Daily Mail*

   C ☐ *The Sun*

4   What are the combined daily sales of *The Times* and the *Financial Times*?

   A ☐ Below one million

   B ☐ Above one million

   C ☐ 1 134 267

5   How many national daily newspapers were sold on average each day of November 2005?

   A ☐ Over 12 million

   B ☐ Close to 6 million

   C ☐ Just 4 million

6   How many daily newspapers sold on average over one million copies per day in November 2005?

   A ☐ 1   **B** ☐ 2   **C** ☐ 3

B5 Reading tables effectively 3

This worksheet accompanies **pages 20–23** in the *Level 2 Skills Book*

Name _____ Date _____

Look at the following table and then answer the questions.

Less Developed Countries (LDCs)			More Developed Countries (MDCs)		
Country	Literacy levels	GDP ppp.	Country	Literacy levels	GDP ppp.
Bangladesh	43	1,100	Australia	99	17,000
Ethiopia	43	470	Germany	99	16,000
Haiti	53	900	Spain	98	13,500
Rwanda	70	790	UK	99	16,000

Comparison of Literacy Rates and GDP in a random selection of LDCs and MDCs

1 From the table, which is the poorest country?

  A ☐ Australia   **B** ☐ Haiti

  C ☐ Spain   **D** ☐ Ethiopia

2 From the table, which is the wealthiest country?

  A ☐ Australia   **B** ☐ Haiti

  C ☐ Spain   **D** ☐ Ethiopia

3 Which LDC has the highest GDP ppp?

  A ☐ Bangladesh   **B** ☐ Ethiopia

  C ☐ Haiti   **D** ☐ Rwanda

4 Which two countries have the same GDP ppp?

  A ☐ Ethiopia and Rwanda   **B** ☐ Bangladesh and Haiti

  C ☐ Australia and Spain   **D** ☐ Germany and UK

5 Which two countries have the lowest literacy levels?

  A ☐ Germany and UK

  B ☐ Spain and Australia

  C ☐ Bangladesh and Ethiopia

  D ☐ Haiti and Rwanda

6 What can you say about the link between a country's wealth and its literacy levels?

  A ☐ Literacy levels have no link with wealth.

  B ☐ The wealthiest countries generally have the highest literacy levels.

  C ☐ Less developed countries have the highest literacy levels.

  D ☐ You can have a wealthy country even if the people can't read and write.

Footnotes

1. *Literacy Rates: Percentage of the population who can read and write by the age of 15.*

2. *GDP ppp: A measure of the country's wealth per person in the country.*

3. *LDCs: Less developed countries – the poorest countries in the world.*

4. *MDCs: More developed countries – the wealthiest countries in the world.*

B6 Conventional language features and presentational features

This worksheet accompanies **pages 16–23** in the *Level 2 Skills Book*

Name _____ Date _____

This table summarises the conventional language features and presentational features in four common text types. Use it as a revision aid to help you answer questions in the test about a specific text's audience and purpose.

Text type	Example	Language features	Presentational features
Information leaflet	Health leaflet warning about the dangers of smoking	■ Written in the third person (e.g. he, she, it) ■ Formal language ■ Simple sentences ■ Carefully structured.	■ Headlines ■ Subheadings ■ Illustrations ■ Columns.
Advertisement	Advertisement to sell a soft drink	■ Addressed specifically to the reader ■ May break grammatical rules ■ Persuasive language: extensive use of adjectives, adverbs ■ Superlatives ■ Imperatives.	■ Bright colours ■ Eye-catching illustrations ■ Possibly a lack of formality ■ Possibly cartoon characters.
Newspaper report	Report on national disaster	■ Written in the third person ■ Formal language ■ Range of sentence structures ■ Emotive language, with extensive use of adjectives and adverbs ■ Carefully structured.	■ Headline ■ Subheadings ■ Columns ■ Picture with caption.
Letter	Letter to travel agent to complain about disastrous holiday	■ Written in first person ■ Formal language ■ Range of sentence structures ■ Well thought out use of adjectives and adverbs ■ Carefully structured.	■ Address ■ Salutation (e.g. Dear Madam) ■ Paragraphs.

C Understanding how writers achieve their purpose

(pages 26–49 in the Skills Book)

Speaking and Listening	Reading	Writing
SLlc2.3 Express clearly statements of fact, explanations, instructions, accounts, descriptions using appropriate structure, style and vocabulary. **SLd2.4** Support opinions and arguments with evidence.	**Rt/2.2** Identify purpose of a text and infer meaning which is not explicit. **Rt/2.7** Use different reading strategies to find and obtain information.	**Wt/2.3** Present ideas in logical / persuasive sequence; use paragraphs where appropriate. **Wt2.5** Use formal and informal language appropriate to purpose and audience. **Wt/2.6** Use different styles of writing for different purposes.

The list indicated above includes the standards covered in the Skills Book and the standards covered in what follows.

Section outline

In Section C students learn to identify a writer's purpose and anticipated audience. By exploring language and presentational features they will become more aware of what writers are trying to achieve.

The section considers the presentational features and language features of the following text types:

- information
- description
- explanation
- persuasive
- argumentative.

Approaches to teaching

In the test, students will be asked about the intended purpose and audience of different texts. Consequently, it is important for them to understand the different conventions associated with different text types.

Whole class tip

Approach some of the tests in this book as whole class activities. Show how you recognise the language and presentational features of a text, and how you can use this information to identify the writer's purpose and intended audience.

Students must be able to identify:

- **words or phrases** that reveal the author's purpose and intended audience
- **presentational features** that reveal the author's purpose and intended audience.

When preparing students for the test it is important to stress that some texts have more than one purpose and more than one audience. For example:

- A text might be informative *and* persuasive, or informative *and* argumentative.
- A text might be aimed at a specific age group *and* a particular interest group.

Encourage students not to make simplistic judgements about purpose and audience, and stress that in the test they are more likely to be asked to comment on the stylistic features of a text than on the presentational features.

Linked Writing and Speaking and Listening activities

This unit will give you the opportunity to target relevant Speaking and Listening and Writing standards using activities such as the following.

Writing

The following writing activities fit well with the reading activities in this unit because they require students to apply their understanding of how writers' intentions influence their choice of language and presentational features.

■ In Section C2 of the Skills Book you read an article about Letitia Hardy who carried out voluntary work in Sri Lanka. Write an article for a teenage magazine **persuading** people that they should devote some time in their lives to carry out voluntary work. *(Wt/2.3; Wt/2.5)*

■ **Describe** a time in your life when you were either frightened or excited. Try to create the scene for your readers, and explain the way you were feeling as thoroughly as possible. *(Wt/2.6)*

Speaking and Listening

■ Prepare a five minute presentation that **informs** an audience of adults how the facilities in your area could be improved for teenagers. You could support your presentation with PowerPoint. *(SLlc2.3; SLd2.4)*

■ In May 2006 teenagers wearing hoodies were banned from the Bluewater Shopping Centre in Kent. Plan a presentation to an audience of adults, in which you **argue** that adults should not judge teenagers because of what they wear. Support your opinions and arguments with evidence. *(SLlc2.3; SLd2.4)*

Photocopiable worksheets

The following photocopiable sheets have been included for section C:

C1 The author's purpose and intended audience

C2 Information text: The 1906 San Francisco Earthquake

C3 Description text: Great Expectations by Charles Dickens

C4 Explanation text: How mobile phones work

C5 Persuasive text: Smoking and your health

C6 Argument text: Dog owners are selfish

The author's purpose and intended audience

This worksheet accompanies **pages 26–29** in the *Level 2 Skills Book*

Name _____   Date _____

Look at the three extracts below. In each case, what purpose does the text have, and who do you think the intended audience is? Choose from the options in the boxes.

Purposes

To describe	To inform	To persuade

Audiences

Adults	Teenagers	School students

1

Can We Make A Difference?	line 1
Politicians tell us that we all have a responsibility to save the planet. But how can we teenagers meet our responsibilities? Here are some sure-fire ways:	line 2 / line 3
■ Recycle your waste. Separate paper, tins and glass and take it all down to your local waste centre.	line 4 / line 5
■ Buy reusable bags from your supermarket.	line 6
■ Make sure that no electrical items are left on standby.	line 7

Purpose _____

Audience _____

2

26 Conway	line 1
Joan lay deep in her bed, her small face submerged in her pillow, her hollow eyes looking out alert and understanding. As ever, she understood more than she shared. As ever, she was in control. Around her, frames of children and grandchildren smiled at her, and she smiled back with the same restraint that she had managed for generations.	line 2 / line 3 / line 4 / line 5 / line 6

Purpose _____

Audience _____

3

An Attack on Our Civil Liberties	line 1
Why should we all have to wear a disgusting uniform? Why is our individuality stolen from us? It is clear that if we are not happy with what is forced upon us we need to fight back. We need to make our case that individual thought is not encouraged by regimenting us in the same drab clothes.	line 2 / line 3 / line 4 / line 5

Purpose _____

Audience _____

C2 Information text

This worksheet accompanies **pages 26–29** in the *Level 2 Skills Book*

Name _____ Date _____

At 5.15 a.m. on 18th April 1906 San Francisco was rocked by an	line 1
earthquake measuring 8.2 on the Richter Scale. Many buildings	line 2
were immediately damaged or destroyed and at 8.14 a.m. a massive	line 3
aftershock hit the city and destroyed many more.	line 4
Worse was to come. Because of broken gas pipes many huge	line 5
fires ripped through the city. Also, some businessmen set fire to	line 6
their damaged property in the belief that they would not receive	line 7
insurance money for earthquake-damaged buildings. The fires burnt	line 8
for four days and caused more damage than the original earthquake.	line 9
In all, it has been estimated that between 3,000 and 6,000 people	line 10
lost their lives. Many were killed by falling buildings. However, the	line 11
Mayor, E. E. Schmitz gave the army and the police permission to	line 12
shoot looters, and at least nine people were killed in this way. In	line 13
addition, there are accounts of people being killed out of mercy if it	line 14
was felt that they were hurt beyond help.	line 15

1 What is the main purpose of this text?

  A ☐ To inform people about the 1906 San Francisco earthquake.

  B ☐ To inform people about Mayor Schmitz.

  C ☐ To inform people that 8.2 on the Richter Scale is extremely dangerous.

  D ☐ To inform business people that they cannot get insurance for earthquake damage.

2 Who is the likely target audience?

  A ☐ People who are worried about earthquakes.

  B ☐ Primary school children.

  C ☐ Teenagers reading a history textbook.

  D ☐ People who want to know what the Richter Scale is.

3 Which of the following pieces of information does **not** appear in the text?

  A ☐ The earthquake hit San Francisco at 5.15 a.m.

  B ☐ The fires burnt for four days.

  C ☐ The earthquake was felt as far away as Los Angeles.

  D ☐ The army and the police shot looters.

4 Which of the following best describes the tone of this text?

  A ☐ Casual and entertaining.

  B ☐ Informative and factual.

  C ☐ Persuasive and emotive.

  D ☐ Descriptive and narrative.

C3 Description text

This worksheet accompanies **pages 30–33** in the *Level 2 Skills Book*

Name _____ Date _____

"Hold your noise!" cried a terrible voice, as a man started up from	line 1
among the graves at the side of the church porch. "Keep still, you little	line 2
devil, or I'll cut your throat!"	line 3
A fearful man, all in coarse grey, with a great iron on his leg. A man	line 4
with no hat, and with broken shoes, and with an old rag tied round	line 5
his head. A man who had been soaked in water, and smothered in	line 6
mud, and lamed by stones, and cut by flints, and stung by nettles, and	line 7
torn by briars; who limped, and shivered, and glared and growled; and	line 8
whose teeth chattered in his head as he seized me by the chin.	line 9
"O! Don't cut my throat, sir," I pleaded in terror. "Pray don't do it, sir."	line 10
"Tell us your name!" said the man. "Quick!"	line 11
"Pip, sir."	line 12
"Once more," said the man, staring at me. "Give it mouth!"	line 13
"Pip. Pip, sir."	line 14
"Show us where you live," said the man. "Pint out the place!"	line 15
I pointed to where our village lay, on the flat in-shore among the	line 16
alder-trees and pollards, a mile or more from the church.	line 17

1 What is the main purpose of this text?

A ☐ To introduce a key character in the novel.

B ☐ To show that Pip was frightened.

C ☐ To show that Pip hung around in graveyards at night.

D ☐ To tell the reader where Pip lived.

2 What does the phrase 'with a great iron on his leg' suggest?

A ☐ That he had polio.

B ☐ That he had been manacled, like a prisoner.

C ☐ That he had been doing the laundry.

D ☐ That he had an artificial leg.

3 The sentence that begins 'A man who had been soaked...' is an unusually long sentence. What effect does its length have?

A ☐ It makes it difficult to read.

B ☐ It makes the reader want to put in some punctuation.

C ☐ It gives the impression that Pip took in lots of details, all at once.

D ☐ It makes Pip sound confused.

C4 Explanation text

This worksheet accompanies **pages 34–37** in the *Level 2 Skills Book*

Name _____ Date _____

Before we look at the mobile phone we need to know how the walkie-	line 1
talkie and CB radio work. The walkie-talkie and CB radio have a lot	line 2
in common, although the CB Radio is much more versatile. When two	line 3
people talk together on a walkie-talkie or a CB radio they share the	line 4
same radio frequency. This means that only one person can talk at	line 5
a time. Walkie-talkies are usually set at their frequency. However, a	line 6
CB radio user can have 40 different frequencies to choose from. This	line 7
means that someone using a CB radio has more choice about who they	line 8
can talk to. Another advantage the CB radio has is its range. Walkie-	line 9
talkies generally have a range of about 1 mile while CB radios often	line 10
have a range of over 5 miles.	line 11

The mobile phone has built on this technology. A mobile phone is really a sophisticated walkie-talkie or CB radio. It has a wider range because the country has been split up into areas called cells. In each cell there is an aerial and transmitter. Each cell is about 10 miles across so there are thousands of aerials and transmitters all over the country. Because so many people use mobile phones in built-up areas more frequencies needed to be provided. In a city there might be as many as 800 frequencies.

```
line 12
line 13
line 14
line 15
line 16
line 17
line 18
line 19
```

1 What is the purpose of this text?

A ☐ To tell readers about the history of the CB radio.

B ☐ To explain what radio frequencies are.

C ☐ To explain why people don't use walkie-talkies any more.

D ☐ To explain how mobile phones work.

2 Which of the following most accurately describes the style of this text?

A ☐ Humorous and entertaining.

B ☐ Persuasive and emotive.

C ☐ Factual and explanatory.

D ☐ Descriptive and atmospheric.

3 What most suggests that this text has been written for an intelligent audience?

A ☐ Its subject matter.   **B** ☐ The technical language.

C ☐ The length.   **D** ☐ It doesn't have any illustrations.

4 Which of the following pieces of information does not appear in the text?

A ☐ Walkie-talkies have a range of about 1 mile.

B ☐ The CB radio is more versatile than the walkie-talkie.

C ☐ Mobile phone cells are about ten miles across.

D ☐ Mobile phone batteries are lighter than walkie-talkie batteries.

C5 Persuasive text

This worksheet accompanies **pages 38–41** in the *Level 2 Skills Book*

Name ______________________ Date __________

One of the most foolish things that you can do as a teenager is smoke. While you walk down the road looking 'oh so cool' you are actually killing yourself. And it's no good saying that your granddad smoked 60 cigarettes a day and lived until he was 80 so obviously smoking is not dangerous. Medical researchers are absolutely definite about the evil effects of smoking.

So, let's look at the health effects. Almost 100,000 people die a painful death every year in Britain because cancer has eaten away their lungs. You shorten your life by 10 years and what you have left is ruined as you gasp for breath, cough up tar every time you move, and find yourself sitting on your own because you smell so bad.

What is more, smoking is ridiculously expensive. At today's prices smoking 20 cigarettes a day for only one year will cost you a whopping £1,500: the cost of two journeys to Australia. So, who's 'oh so cool' now?

Give up smoking immediately. Don't finish your last packet, throw it away. Save money. Save your life.

1 What is the purpose of this text?

A ☐ To inform people about the dangers of smoking.

B ☐ To persuade teenage smokers to give up the habit.

C ☐ To argue that smoking is not dangerous.

D ☐ To describe what it is like to smoke a cigarette.

2 Which people might the text be aimed at?

A ☐ Health experts　　**B** ☐ Adult smokers

C ☐ Teenage smokers　　**D** ☐ Teachers

3 Which of the following phrases is emotive?

A ☐ Let's look at the health effects.

B ☐ Your granddad smoked 60 cigarettes a day.

C ☐ Don't finish your last packet.

D ☐ Because cancer has eaten away your lungs.

4 Which of the following words would best replace the word "ridiculously" in the sentence "What is more, smoking is ridiculously expensive."?

A ☐ quite　　**B** ☐ not

C ☐ foolishly　　**D** ☐ extremely

5 Which of the following phrases best describes the style of this text?

A ☐ Factual and well balanced

B ☐ Informative and honest

C ☐ Persuasive and emotive

D ☐ Descriptive and narrative

C6 Argument text

This worksheet accompanies **pages 42–45** in the *Level 2 Skills Book*

Name _____   Date _____

Many dog owners will give the impression that they are doing their pets a favour by	line 1
looking after them, but in my view dog owners are selfish and have pets because they	line 2
are easier to look after than children.	line 3
The dog is an extremely obedient animal, which is happiest when its owner is pleased	line 4
with its behaviour. That is why it is so easy to train dogs – they want to please. This	line 5
is in sharp contrast to children who are extremely selfish, and are happiest when their	line 6
own needs are satisfied. Consequently, a dog can be treated badly but accept all of	line 7
the blame, and come back to its owner trying even harder to please. This makes dog	line 8
owners feel powerful and important. Bringing up children requires much more thought	line 9
and care, and parents will feel that they never get enough appreciation from their	line 10
children. This makes parents feel inadequate.	line 11
It could be argued that another reason people have dogs is because dogs don't hold	line 12
grudges. When a dog owner is feeling frustrated he or she can shout at their dog	line 13
knowing that their dog will cower for a minute or two, but then will come back later	line 14
and grovel to their owners. However, if parents shout at children, children are likely	line 15
to sulk for days, and in the end it is the parents who have to grovel. Consequently,	line 16
owning a dog is much less effort than bringing up children as dog owners only have	line 17
to think about themselves, while parents have to think about their children as well.	line 18

1 What is the main purpose of this text?

   A ☐ To argue that dogs are cleverer than children.

   B ☐ To argue that children are ungrateful.

   C ☐ To argue that dog owners are selfish.

   D ☐ To argue that parents shouldn't have dogs as well as children.

2 What phrase would best describe the tone of this text?

   A ☐ Persuasive and factual

   B ☐ Argumentative and humorous

   C ☐ Descriptive and emotional

   D ☐ Explanatory and factual

3 Which word would best replace the word "extremely" in the phrase
   "The dog is an extremely obedient animal..."?

   A ☐ somewhat   **B** ☐ unusually

   C ☐ unsurprisingly   **D** ☐ exceptionally

4 Which of the following best expresses the main point of view of the
   author of this text?

   A ☐ Children are selfish.

   B ☐ Dogs make excellent pets.

   C ☐ Owning a dog is easier than bringing up children.

   D ☐ Dogs don't hold grudges.

D Spelling

(pages 50–59 in the Skills Book)

Speaking and Listening	Reading	Writing
SLc2.1 Speak clearly and confidently in a way which suits the occasion.	**RW/2.1** Read and understand technical vocabulary. **RW/2.2** Use reference materials to find meanings of unfamiliar words.	**Wt/2.1** Plan and draft writing. **Ww/2.1** Spell correctly, including familiar technical words. **Wt/2.7** Proof read and revise.

The list indicated above includes the standards covered in the Skills Book and the standards covered in what follows.

Section outline

Section D covers a range of spelling skills that will help performance in the Adult Literacy test. Students will learn about:

- ▣ spelling rules
- ▣ spelling strategies.

Approaches to teaching

You will need to teach two important concepts in this section:

- ▣ That there is a great deal of regularity in English spelling.
- ▣ Learning rules and strategies can improve spelling.

Encourage students to overcome any fears they have about their spelling. Provide them with opportunities to succeed.

Whole class tip

Ask the students to mark the spelling in a piece of their own extended writing, calculating how many of the first 100 words they spelt correctly. This should emphasise that most people spell correctly most of the words that they use.
It is not very productive to have whole class spelling lessons. This is because different students will have problems with different rules. Consequently, to improve spelling you need to work with individual students and their specific problems.

Some suggested approaches

- ▣ When you are marking students' work, do not underline every single spelling mistake that they make. Target mark. That is, try to identify patterns

of spelling errors in a student's writing and target one such pattern at a time. For example, a student may make mistakes with adding some prefixes and some suffixes. Choose one pattern, such as 'when to drop the e', and when this has been mastered choose another pattern, such as 'changing y to i'.

- ▣ Students are required to learn a great deal of subject specific vocabulary. Produce spelling lists of specialist vocabulary that your students have to learn, and give them regular tests of ten words from these lists.

- ▣ Most of a student's spelling mistakes will be the same words regularly spelt incorrectly. Encourage students to make a list of the words that they regularly spell incorrectly. For example, mistakes with *your* and *you're*, *to* and *too*, and *there* and *their* are commonly cited by Chief Examiners as common, but careless, spelling errors.

- ▣ Teach students how to guess the first few letters of difficult words and then use a dictionary to find the correct spelling.

- ▣ Above all, encourage the students to take responsibility for their own spelling, and do not allow them to say that they can't spell.

Linked Writing and Speaking and Listening activities

This unit will give you the opportunity to target relevant Speaking and Listening and Writing standards using activities such as the following.

Speaking and Listening

- ▣ Ask a student to call a word out to the class. Ask the next student to give a word that begins with the last letter of the first word. Go around the class asking each student to give a word that begins with the last letter of the previous word. *(SLc2.1)*

- When students feel confident with this game, ask them to give words that begin with the penultimate letter of the previous word. *(SLc2.1)*

- Split the class into two teams. Each team should challenge the other to spell a word. Points are scored when a team cannot spell a word but the challenging team can. *(SLc2.1)*

Writing

- Play Hangman, focusing on words that students regularly spell incorrectly. *(Ww2.1)*

- Split the class into two teams. Provide one team with the word **astronaut** and the other with **cosmonaut**. Challenge the students to make as many four or more letter words using the letters in their given word. *(Ww2.1)*

- Provide the students with a piece of text on a topical issue that you have prepared, but make ten spelling errors in the text. The students should identify the errors and correct them. *(Ww2.1, Wt2.7)*

- The students should use ICT to make displays of subject specific vocabulary that they need to learn. *(Ww2.1)*

- The students should use ICT to make displays of words that are commonly misspelt. *(Ww2.1)*

- The students should regularly go through work that the teacher has marked, and make lists of the words that are regularly spelt incorrectly. *(Ww2.1, Wt2.7)*

- In pairs, students should mark each other's work to identify spelling errors. *(Ww2.1, Wt2.7)*

Spelling challenge!

Here are 50 words your students could check they know how to spell.

Literacy	Numeracy	ICT	Humanities	Science
Image	Statistic	Technology	Civilisation	Extinct
Media	Geometry	Appearance	Reference	Muscle
Audience	Multiply	Analyse	Government	Nuclear
Formal	Subtract	Processor	Parliament	Electricity
Informal	Addition	Presentation	Agriculture	Classify
Quotation	Percentage	Graphics	Archaeology	Habitat
Literature	Diagonal	Logo	Abolish	Soluble
Scene	Decimal	Implement	Population	Skeleton
Apostrophe	Triangle	Adjust	Country	Experiment
Comment	Centre	Document	Village	Bacteria

Photocopiable worksheets

The following photocopiable sheets have been included for section D:

D1 Plurals

D2 Homophones

D3 Prefixes

D4 Suffixes

D5 Spelling test 1

D6 Spelling test 2

D1 Plurals

This worksheet accompanies **pages 52–53** in the *Level 2 Skills Book*

Name _____   Date _____

1 In each sentence below, circle the correct spelling in the brackets.

   A In the cave I could hear a mass of (echoes / echos).

   B There were three (knifes / knives) in the kitchen sink.

   C How many (glass / glasses) should I put on the table?

   D Which four (countrys / countries) make up the United Kingdom?

   E (Calves / calfs) usually stay close to their mothers.

   F The pavement was covered in fallen (leaves / leafs).

2 Can you spell the plurals of the following words?

Singular	Plural
party	
pencil	
dictionary	
church	
gas	
half	
piano	
fox	

3 In this passage six plurals have been spelt incorrectly. Identify the incorrectly spelt words, and then correct them.

Janna walked cautiously into the publisher's office and looked around.	line 1
On the desk, very neatly laid out, there were three photoes of young	line 2
babys, three penciles, two pens, and a clock. There were two boxs of	line 3
dictionarys on the window sill, ready to be sent off to customers. The	line 4
shelfs bent under the weight of hundreds of reference books. Behind	line 5
the desk two attractive ladys in suits smiled warmly. Janna hoped	line 6
that she would be offered a job here.	line 7

Mistakes	Corrections

D2 Homophones

This worksheet accompanies **pages 54–55** in the *Level 2 Skills Book*

Name _____   Date _____

Homophones are words that sound the same but are spelt differently.

1 In the following passage the writer has used the wrong homophone seven times. Can you identify the seven errors and correct them?

It was Hilary's birthday and she was weighting impatiently for the male to	line 1
be delivered, as she was expecting at least for cards. Won card, from her	line 2
friend Dione, would contain a letter with a hole lot of news from California.	line 3
A letter from her Auntie Sandra, should have sum money in it. The other too	line 4
cards were from her grandparents and were also likely to contain money.	line 5

Mistakes	Corrections

2 In each sentence below, circle the correct spelling in the brackets.

A You can go to jail if you (steal / steel) other people's property.

B Would you like some stilton (sauce / source) with your steak?

C She (war/wore) a blonde wig to the Christmas party.

D (Wood / would) you like another cup of tea?

E After the crash one of the cars had to be (toad / towed) to the garage.

F Unfortunately, the last (peace/piece) of the jigsaw was missing.

3 Use the clues below to help you to spell the homophones of the following words.

	Clues	Homophones
rain	A king's rule	
pain	Window glass	
story	Floor in a block of flats	
key	Where ships dock	
ball	Cry out loud	
heard	Cows	

D3 Prefixes

This worksheet accompanies **pages 56–57** in the *Level 2 Skills Book*

Name _____   Date _____

A prefix is a group of letters that can be added to the front of a root word. The prefix and the root word form a different word with a different meaning.

1   Match each prefix with a word and write out the new word.

Prefix		Word		New word
re		weight		
dis		wanted		
under		play		
over		polite		
im		visible		
un		ground		
in		appear		

2   Circle the words in the brackets that are spelt correctly.

A   We may lose today because we have such an (unexperienced / inexperienced) team.

B   The window didn't fit because the measurements had been (unaccurate / inaccurate).

C   The examination results were (unexpected / inexpected).

D   He was so (undecisive / indecisive) that I couldn't get him to make up his mind.

E   She was so (impolite / unpolite) that she wouldn't ever say sorry, even when it was clearly her fault.

F   Running that fast for the whole 1500 m race would be (unpossible / impossible).

3   Match up the prefixes with their meanings by drawing a line from each prefix to a meaning.

Prefix		Meaning
re		three
mis		again
tri		before
pre		not
un		after
post		wrong

Suffixes

This worksheet accompanies **pages 56–57** in the *Level 2 Skills Book*

Name _____   Date _____

A suffix is a group of letters that can be added to the end of a root word. The suffix and the root word form a different word with a different meaning.

1 Complete these sentences by circling the correct words in the brackets.

   A Ben was (runing / running) down the road to try to catch the bus.

   B It was such a (sunny / suny) day that driving a car became difficult.

   C The water was (pumped / pumpd) out of the flooded house and into the road.

   D I have always enjoyed (travelling / traveling) at home and abroad.

   E Grandad (treated / treatted) all of his grandchildren to a day at Alton Towers.

2 In the following passage there are ten spelling mistakes. Each of the mistakes involves adding a suffix to a root word. Correct these mistakes.

Sebastian Coe, who headded the team that brought the 2012 Summer Olympics to London, is well qualifyed for the job. He has set eight world records and won four Olympic medals in middle distance runing. Coe also studyed economics at Loughborough University.	line 1 line 2 line 3 line 4
Through the late 1970s and early 1980s Sebastian Coe, and his British rival Steve Ovett, dominatted 800 m and 1500 m running. They traveled all over the world to race against each other, benefitting from their rivalry.	line 5 line 6 line 7
After retirring from running Sebastian Coe has an opportunity to put something back into athletics. He is Chairperson of the London Organissing Committee of the Olympic Games. It is this Committee that has to ensure that the 2012 Olympic Games in London are succesful.	line 8 line 9 line 10 line 11

Mistake	Correction
headded	
qualifyed	
runing	
studyed	
dominatted	
traveled	
benefitting	
retirring	
Organissing	
succesful	

D5 Spelling test 1

Name _____   Date _____

Read this book review and then answer the questions below.

Gangsta Rap by Benjamin Zephaniah   line 1

This is a novel that everyone should read. It is full of excitement and action,   line 2
and everything seems to be so _____. Ray is a fifteen year old who   line 3
has lost interest in school and is frequently in trouble. When he and his two   line 4
friends are excluded from _____ school they all agree to attend a Social   line 5
Inclusion Project, _____ the curriculum meets their particular interests.   line 6
The boys form their own rap group called Positive Negatives. _____,   line 7
as the band becomes more popular it gets involved in gang warfare with   line 8
another London rap band, The Western Alliance.   line 9

The characters in this novel are convincing, and the twist at the end is   line 10
unexpected. I couldnt put the novel down, and I would _____ it to   line 11
anyone interested in what teenagers can _____ if they try hard enough.   line 12

---

1   What is the correct word to complete line 3?

   A ☐ realistick   **B** ☐ realistic   **C** ☐ reallistic

2   What is the correct spelling of the word missing in line 5?

   A ☐ they're   **B** ☐ there   **C** ☐ their

3   Which of the following words fills the gap in line 6
   correctly?

   A ☐ were   **B** ☐ wear   **C** ☐ where

4   Which of the following words completes line 7 correctly?

   A ☐ Unfortunately   **B** ☐ Unfortunattely

   C ☐ Unfortunatly

5   What is wrong with the spelling of 'couldn't' in line 11?

   A ☐ It should be 'could of'.

   B ☐ It should be 'could'.

   C ☐ There should be an apostrophe between 'n' and 't'.

6   Which of the following words completes line 11 correctly?

   A ☐ recommend **B** ☐ recomend   **C** ☐ recumend

7   Which of the following words completes line 12 correctly?

   A ☐ acheive   **B** ☐ achieve   **C** ☐ acheeve

D6 Spelling test 2

This worksheet accompanies **pages 50–59** in the *Level 2 Skills Book*

Name _____   Date _____

Read the passage and then answer the questions below.

Many dog owners will give the impression that they are doing their	line 1
pets a _____ by looking after them, but in my view dog owners	line 2
have pets because they are _____ to look after than children.	line 3
The dog is an extremely obedient animal, which is _____ when	line 4
its owner is pleased with its _____. That is why it is so easy to	line 5
train dogs – they want to please. This is in sharp contrast to children	line 6
who are extremely selfish, and are happiest when their own needs are	line 7
satisfied. _____, a dog can be treated badly but accept all of the	line 8
blame, and come back to its owner trying even harder to please. This	line 9
makes dog owners feel _____ and important. Bringing up children	line 10
requires much more thought and care, and parents will feel that they	line 11
never get enough appreciation from _____ children. This makes	line 12
parents feel inadequate.	line 13
So, if you had to make a choice between a child or a dog _____	line 14
would you choose?	line 15

1 Which of the following words fills the gap in line 2 correctly?

A ☐ favour   B ☐ favor   C ☐ faver

2 Which of the following words fills the gap in line 3 correctly?

A ☐ easier   B ☐ eesier   C ☐ easyer

3 Which of the following words fills the gap in line 4 correctly?

A ☐ happyest   B ☐ happyist   C ☐ happiest

4 Which of the following words fills the gap in line 5 correctly?

A ☐ behaviour B ☐ behavior   C ☐ behaviur

5 Which of the following words fills the gap in line 8 correctly?

A ☐ Concequently   B ☐ Consequentely

C ☐ Consequently

6 Which of the following words fills the gap in line 10 correctly?

A ☐ powerfull B ☐ powerful   C ☐ powerful

7 Which of the following words fills the gap in line 12 correctly?

A ☐ there   B ☐ they're   C ☐ their

8 Which of the following words fills the gap in line 14 correctly?

A ☐ witch   B ☐ which   C ☐ wich

E Punctuation

(pages 60–73 in the Skills Book)

Speaking and Listening	Reading	Writing
SLc/2.1 Speak clearly and confidently in a way which suits the situation.	**Rt/2.6** Use organisational features and systems to locate texts and information.	**Wt/2.1** Plan and draft writing. **Ws/2.4** Punctuate sentences correctly. **Wt/2.7** Proof read and revise.

The list indicated above includes the standards covered in the Skills Book and the standards covered in what follows.

Section outline

Section E helps students to improve their punctuation. It also covers the following punctuation skills that will be assessed in the Adult Literacy test:

- sentence construction
- use of commas
- apostrophe of omission and possession
- inverted commas
- paragraphing.

Approaches to teaching

You will need to teach two important concepts in this section:

- punctuation is used to remove ambiguity in writing.
- all students can improve their use of punctuation.

Whole class tip

Whole class teaching of punctuation is very effective. Students learn by seeing punctuation choices being modelled by a teacher. Modelling also provides the teacher with an opportunity to explain the effects that individual pieces of punctuation have. Write a paragraph on the board, and explain why you have used capital letters and full stops. Explain why subordinate clauses have been isolated with commas. Explain why the apostrophe of omission or possession has been used.

As students become more confident they should be able to do the following:

- identify what punctuation marks have been omitted from pieces of writing
- identify errors in the use of punctuation
- explain what purpose a piece of punctuation serves.

It is not enough for students to be able to use punctuation – they also need to understand the effects punctuation has.

Some suggested approaches

- Punctuation helps to remove ambiguity in a piece of writing. Provide students with passages of writing that have no punctuation. Illustrate how difficult it is to read writing that has not been punctuated. In groups, the students can punctuate these passages to learn how important punctuation is.

- There are specific punctuation rules that students need to learn. These rules range from the most basic rules about the use of capital letters to the more complicated use of the apostrophe of possession.

- However, students also need to understand that different writers can make different punctuation choices. For example, writers can choose when to use the exclamation mark. Also, a passage of writing can be paragraphed in a number of different ways.

Linked Speaking and Listening and Writing activities

This unit will give you the opportunity to forget relevant Speaking and Listening and Writing standards, using activities such as the following.

Writing

- Work with the class to produce a piece of collaborative writing. For example, write the first paragraph of an essay with the title 'The school leaving age should be raised to 18'. During this exercise stress to the students how important punctuation is. It removes ambiguity. It can also be used to emphasise particular words or ideas. *(Wt2.1, Ws2.4, Wt2.7)*

- Provide the students with a piece of continuous prose that has not been paragraphed. Ask the students to indicate where they think each paragraph should start. *(Ws2.4, Wt2.7)*

- Each student should choose a piece of text from a book or magazine. The students should type out their chosen passage omitting all punctuation. They should then challenge each other to replace the punctuation. *(Ws2.4, Wt2.7)*

Speaking and listening

- In pairs, students should mark each other's work to identify punctuation errors.

- In pairs, students should take turns to read out a piece of text while their partner has to say which punctuation marks would be used and where they would go. *(SLc2.1)*

- On the board, define the structure of a sentence that you would like the students to write. In the following example the gaps represent words:

  _____ _____ _____ _____ _____.
  ____, _____, _____ _____ ____ ____!

  The students should make suggestions about what sentence could be created to fit that structure. To help the students a subject could be defined, such as 'The value of regular physical exercise'. *(SLc 2.1)*

Photocopiable worksheets

The following photocopiable worksheets have been included for Section E:

E1 Sentence punctuation

E2 Commas

E3 Apostrophes

E4 Inverted commas

E5 Paragraphs

E6 Punctuation test.

E1 Sentence punctuation

This worksheet accompanies **pages 60–61** in the *Level 2 Skills Book*

Name _____ Date _____

1 Match up each of the sentences in the first column with one of the sentence types in the second column.

	Sentences
A	How long ago did you have your hair cut?
B	Go and get your hair cut immediately!
C	Your hair has been cut.
D	You've had your hair cut!

Sentence types
Statement
Question
Exclamation
Command

2 Read the following sentences and add the necessary capital letters and punctuation.

A do you think that razorlight's new cd is better than their first one

B i must remember to send a card to my friend in france

C help help

D i would like to go to nottingham university next year

E would you like to come to town with me tonight

F just sit there and shut up

3 Read this draft document and then answer the questions underneath.

Do you think that this is a true story or not. On 14th June 1531 Elizabeth	line 1
Hurshaw got married in Daglingworth, Gloucestershire. Most of the guests	line 2
were invited back. To her house where she organised a game of hide and	line 3
seek. When it was her turn to hide she hid in a very old oak chest that	line 4
was kept in a rarely used room, her hiding place was a very successful one	line 5
because after an hour nobody had found her. Losing interest in the game	line 6
she tried to lift the heavy oak lid, but unfortunately she wasn't strong	line 7
enough. The guests searched for elizabeth for four days, and there were	line 8
countless rumours about her disappearance. It wasn't until 14th June 1534	line 9
that her body was found in the very old oak chest.	line 10

a) In which line should a question mark have been used?

A ☐ line 1 **B** ☐ line 5 **C** ☐ line 6 **D** ☐ line 8

b) What is wrong with the following: 'To her house where she organised a game of hide and seek.'?

A ☐ It isn't true.

B ☐ It should have a question mark at the end.

C ☐ It is not a sentence.

D ☐ The word 'she' should have a capital letter.

c) On which line has a comma been used when a full stop should have been used?

A ☐ line 2 **B** ☐ line 5 **C** ☐ line 6 **D** ☐ line 7

 Commas

This worksheet accompanies **pages 62–63** in the *Level 2 Skills Book*

Name _____   Date _____

1 Write why commas are used in each of the sentences in the table below:
- to separate items in a list
- to separate out additional information
- to separate clauses.

	Sentences	Why are the commas used?
A	Would you like a cup of tea, a cup of coffee, a glass of orange or a glass of milk?	
B	Esther kept trying to get some work done, but she had to keep answering the telephone.	
C	It was Sunday, the quietest day of the week, when she went missing.	
D	Charlotte was a very hard worker, driven by a desire to get everything done to the best of her ability.	
E	Before I go out tonight I need to do my homework, pack my bag for tomorrow, iron a t-shirt and find my shoes.	
F	Although Maddie saw how untidy her room was, she sat down and turned the television on.	

2 Read the following sentences and then add the necessary commas.

A Today I went to town and bought three bright shirts a pair of brown shoes a blue and red tie and a box of handkerchiefs.

B Yesterday after I finished all of my work I went to the cinema.

C Although Harriet was hungry she refused to eat because she was on a diet.

D To get to Taunton from here you need to go down this road for two miles turn left at the crossroads continue for about a hundred yards turn left at the t-junction then continue for about four miles. It's easy.

E It was a dark night the darkest night for ages and Dean was scared.

F Lucy spilt beer down her dress completely ruining it.

G Jo bought some fresh fruit from the supermarket then she went straight home.

H When I was younger much younger I lived in Holland.

I In my opinion for what it's worth everyone should try to save some money every month.

J My favourite meal is rib-eye steak sauté potatoes mushrooms battered onions and peas.

E3 Apostrophes

This worksheet accompanies **pages 64–67** in the *Level 2 Skills Book*

Name _____ Date _____

1 Write out the shortened forms of each of the following, putting the apostrophe in its correct place. The first one has been done for you.

	Phrases	Shortened forms
1	Should have	Should've
2	Could have	
3	We are	
4	You are	
5	Is not	
6	It is	
7	Could not	
8	Would not	

2 Underline the words in the sentences below that should have apostrophes. Then write them out, placing the apostrophe of possession in its correct place each time.

A Janes sister was going to visit today.

_____

B Its freezing outside.

_____

C Bill crashed his car because the cars tyres were so worn.

_____

D The mens changing room is being decorated.

_____

E The brothers bedroom was really too small for them.

_____

F The English teachers office was designed to fit them all in.

_____

G Calvins and Roberts exercise books have gone missing.

_____

E4 Inverted commas

This worksheet accompanies **pages 68–69** in the *Level 2 Skills Book*

Name _____ Date _____

Read this short extract from a student's piece of writing. She has had some trouble with using inverted commas. Then answer the questions.

Will the visit to the theme park tomorrow last all day? asked Kofi.	line 1 / line 2
Nadine replied Yes, we won't get back until late in the afternoon.'	line 3 / line 4
Good said Kofi. Then I will make a packed lunch for us both. Is there anything that you would especially like?	line 5 / line 6
Nadine smiled. 'That's easy,' she said. 'Just pack lots of chocolate!' 'OK,' answered Kofi. 'I'll see you at 9 o'clock tomorrow morning at the coach station.'	line 7 / line 8 / line 9

1 How should the first sentence of this conversation be punctuated?

A ☐ 'Will the visit to the theme park tomorrow last all day? asked Kofi.'

B ☐ 'Will the visit to the theme park tomorrow last all day'? asked Kofi.

C ☐ 'Will the visit to the theme park tomorrow last all day?' asked Kofi.

D ☐ Will the visit to the theme park tomorrow last all day? asked Kofi.

2 What two pieces of punctuation, and in what order, are missing between replied and Yes in line 3?

A ☐ An explanation mark and a full stop

B ☐ An inverted comma and a comma

C ☐ A full stop and an inverted comma

D ☐ A comma and an inverted comma

3 How should Good said Kofi in line 5 be written?

A ☐ 'Good said Kofi' **B** ☐ 'Good,' said Kofi.

C ☐ 'Good', said Kofi. **D** ☐ Good, 'said Kofi.

4 What mistake has been made on lines 7–9?

A ☐ There shouldn't be a comma after easy in 'That's easy,'

B ☐ The inverted commas after easy and before Just aren't needed

C ☐ The exclamation mark should be placed outside the inverted comma

D ☐ A new line should have been started with 'OK,'

E5 Paragraphs

This worksheet accompanies **pages 70–71** in the *Level 2 Skills Book*

Name _____   Date _____

Read the following article about bullying. There should have been four different paragraphs but the writer forgot to put them in.

Bullying	line 1
Most of us have experienced bullying at one time or another. It can take many	line 2
different forms including verbal abuse, physical abuse and even emotional abuse. But	line 3
why do people bully, and who do they bully? More importantly, what can we do when	line 4
we are being bullied? Bullies are very often people who have already been bullied	line 5
themselves. They might even have been abused by their parents when they were	line 6
younger. They tend to be stronger and more aggressive than other people of their own	line 7
age, and usually they have no regrets about their behaviour. Bullies usually pick on	line 8
children who are weaker, or smaller, or who do not retaliate when they are bullied. The	line 9
bully picks on someone to get rid of their own frustrations. So, what can you do if you	line 10
are being bullied? First of all, keep away from the bully, and keep away from deserted	line 11
places where you might be bullied. Try to hang around with other people. It might be	line 12
possible to stand up to the bully, even though you probably think that this will make	line 13
things worse. Most importantly, tell an adult because they will be able to help.	line 14

1   Where do you think the second paragraph should start?

A ☐   'But why...' on line 3

B ☐   'More importantly...' on line 4

C ☐   'Bullies are...' on line 5

D ☐   'They might...' on line 6

2   Where do you think the third paragraph should start?

A ☐   'They might even...' on line 6

B ☐   'They tend...' on line 7

C ☐   'Bullies usually...' on line 8

D ☐   'The bully...' on line 9

3   Where do you think the final paragraph should start?

A ☐   'The bully...' on line 9

B ☐   'So, what can...' on line 10

C ☐   First of all...' on line 11

D ☐   'Try to...' on line 12

4   What would be the best title for this article?

A ☐   Reasons why bullies do what they do

B ☐   What can be done when you're being bullied?

C ☐   Understanding bullying and dealing with it

D ☐   Why some people are bullied

E6 Punctuation test

This worksheet accompanies **pages 60–73** in the *Level 2 Skills Book*

Name _____ Date _____

Read this letter carefully and then answer the questions below.

Dear Sir,	line 1
I recently spent four days at your hotel. And I feel it necessary to write to you to tell you what a wonderful time I had.	line 2 line 3
From the moment my friends and I arrived we were made to feel welcome by your staff. We were booked in very quickly, shown to our rooms and we were told about all of the excellent facilities that you offer. I have to say the meals were as good as the staff said they would be.	line 4 line 5 line 6
The room's were very comfortable. I was delighted to see how they were cleaned spotlessly every day, and the complimentary coffee and biscuit's were appreciated. Your hotel is situated in an amazing place for a holiday. While we were there we went water skiing kayaking fishing speed boat racing and had an opportunity to go on a jet ski. What more could you want on holiday.	line 7 line 8 line 9 line 10 line 11
Because of the situation, the facilities, and your staff's efficiency, we will definitely be back again.	line 12 line 13
Yours sincerely,	line 14
Martin Hammersley	line 15
Martin Hammersley.	line 16

1 What correction is required on line 2?

A ☐ Change days to days' **B** ☐ Change days to day's

C ☐ Change the full stop to a comma and change 'And' to 'and'

D ☐ Change the full stop to a question mark

2 On which lines are there errors in the use of the apostrophe of possession?

A ☐ lines 7 and 8   **B** ☐ lines 8 and 12

C ☐ lines 7 and 12   **D** ☐ lines 4 and 12

3 Where should a new paragraph have been started?

A ☐ line 4   **B** ☐ line 6

C ☐ line 8   **D** ☐ line 10

4 On which line are there commas missing?

A ☐ line 5   **B** ☐ line 7

C ☐ line 9   **D** ☐ line 12

5 What punctuation mark is missing on line 11?

A ☐ a question mark   **B** ☐ a comma

C ☐ a capital letter   **D** ☐ an exclamation mark

F Grammar

(pages 74–83 in the Skills Book)

Speaking and Listening	Reading	Writing
SLc/2.3 Express clearly statements of fact etc. using appropriate structure, style and vocabulary.	**Rt/2.6** Use organizational features and systems to locate texts and information.	**Ws/2.1** Construct complex sentences. **Ws/2.2** Use correct grammar. **Ws/2.3** Use pronouns so meaning is clear.

The list indicated above includes the standards covered in the Skills Book and the standards covered in what follows.

Unit outline

Section F helps students to improve their grammar.

It also covers a range of skills that will be assessed in the Adult Literacy test:

- using connectives
- using the correct tense
- ensuring subject-verb agreement
- using pronouns clearly.

Approaches to teaching

Students will find all of the subjects covered in this unit useful. Even the most proficient students can extend their understanding of grammar, so the subjects covered in this section lend themselves to whole class teaching.

Whole class tip

Students should keep a careful record of all of the work they do in this section. Their work will serve as a valuable reference source for their revision.

In the test students will be asked to do the following:

- identify the most appropriate connectives.
- identify grammatical errors.

Some suggested approaches

Whole class tip

Whole class teaching of grammar is very effective. Students will learn from the examples that they consider together and will start to think about the clarity of their writing.

- Connectives help to make logical links between *ideas* within a paragraph. They also help to make logical links between *paragraphs*. Effective use of connectives helps readers see the intellectual cohesion within a piece of writing. To encourage the students to use a range of connectives ask them to make a record of connectives that they come across in their own reading.

- Students frequently select an inappropriate tense for the verbs that they are using. They also make frequent subject-verb agreement errors. These errors are rarely related to a lack of understanding; they are more likely to be as a result of careless drafting. When students are redrafting tell them to check their grammar as well as their spelling and punctuation.

- Chief examiners complain that students often confuse the reader through their overuse of pronouns. Students regularly cause this confusion because they take it for granted that the reader has the same understanding of their subject as the writer has. It is important to explain to students the degree of ambiguity that poor use of pronouns can cause.

Linked Speaking and Listening and Writing activities

This unit will give you the opportunity to target relevant Speaking and Listening and Writing standards, using activities such as the following.

Writing

■ Model a piece of extended writing. Explain how you achieve the internal logic of your writing by using appropriate connectives. Show how some connectives are more appropriate than others.

■ Provide a piece of writing in the present tense. The students should explain how they would change the text in order to present it in the past tense.

■ Provide categories of connectives, such as comparing, persuading and concluding. The students should add connectives to each of these categories.

■ Students should deliberately write sentences in which the verbs and tense do not agree. They should then challenge other students to correct the sentences.

■ Students should deliberately write sentences in which the subjects and verbs do not agree. They should then challenge other students to correct the sentences.

■ Students should deliberately write sentences in which ambiguity has been created because of the overuse of pronouns. They should then challenge other students to correct the sentences.

Speaking and listening

■ As a starter, provide sentences in which the subjects and verbs do not agree. The students should recommend improvements to the sentences.

■ As a starter, provide sentences that are ambiguous because of the overuse of pronouns. The students should identify different possible interpretations.

Photocopiable worksheets

The following photocopiable sheets are included for Section F:

F1 Connectives

F2 Tenses

F3 Subject-verb agreement

F4 Using pronouns

F5 Grammar test 1

F6 Grammar test 2

F1 Connectives

This worksheet accompanies **pages 74–75** in the *Level 2 Skills Book*

Name _____   Date _____

1 Place the following connectives in the correct categories in the table below. Afterwards, add a connective of your own to each category.

| First | However | Above all | Therefore | For example | Finally |

Indeed

For instance   As a result   Ultimately   Next   Meanwhile

Sequencing:	Cause and effect:
Contrasting:	**Illustrating:**
Emphasising:	**Concluding:**

2 Choose the appropriate connectives from Question 1 to complete the following passage.

When I leave school I would like to become famous. [1]_____ I want to get a good education. [2]_____ I want to start my own company. [3]_____, I could study general building and then set up my own building company. [4]_____, this is not the only possibility. [5]_____, there is an infinite number of possibilities.

F2 Tenses

This worksheet accompanies **pages 76–77** in the *Level 2 Skills Book*

Name _____   Date _____

1 Read the following e-mail from Pat to her friend. Circle the
correct choice each time that you are given an option.

Dear Mo,	line 1
I am delighted to hear that you had/ have arrived back safely from your stay with me.	line 2
I had/have a wonderful time and I hope that you will/did too. I particularly enjoyed/	line 3
will enjoy the day that we spent at Woolacombe. I did/didn't realise that you could	line 4
surf so well. I also enjoyed the trip to London where we visited/did visit so many	line 5
shops.	line 6
I looked forward/look forward to returning the visit and spending some time with	line 7
you next year at your house. I hope/hoped that you will have some exciting days out	line 8
planned for us both.	line 9
Love	line 10
Pat	line 11

2 Read the following article that appeared in an American
newspaper. Afterwards, answer the questions about the
article.

Ian McEwan risked his life yesterday in order to save the life of a complete stranger.	line 1
While working at the Bodie Campsite in California, McEwan hears a woman's scream.	line 2
He stopped what he was doing and immediately ran towards the scream. What he	line 3
saw made his heart freeze. Angela Ash <u>lies</u> in a pool of her own blood, a huge brown	line 4
bear looming over her, <u>gnawed</u> at her left leg. Without a thought for himself McEwan	line 5
grabbed a nearby log and beat the bear away. Afterwards the brave campsite worker	line 6
said, 'Wow! That was close. I've never had to fight with a bear before.' Last night	line 7
Angela Ash was reported to be comfortable in hospital.	line 8

  A Has this newspaper article been written in

  A ☐ the past tense

  B ☐ the present tense

  C ☐ the future tense

  B Which word in line 2 is in the wrong tense?

  A ☐ while **B** ☐ working **C** ☐ hears

  C The word underlined in line 4 is the wrong tense.
  What word should have been used?

  A ☐ lied **B** ☐ lay **C** ☐ laid

  D The word underlined in line 5 is the wrong tense.
  What word should have been used?

  A ☐ gnaws **B** ☐ gnaw **C** ☐ gnawing

F3 Subject-verb agreement

This worksheet accompanies **pages 78–79** in the *Level 2 Skills Book*

Name _____   Date _____

1   All of the following sentences are in the present tense. Write the correct verbs in the spaces and make sure that the subjects and verbs agree.

   A   Abdul and Karim _____ going to go to the cinema this evening.

   B   They _____ the tickets for tonight's show.

   C   She _____ the most intelligent person I have ever met.

   D   I am sure that they _____ win this afternoon.

   E   If you _____ looking for me I will be down town somewhere.

   F   None of the girls _____ allowed to go out tonight.

2   Read this advertisement that appeared in a teenage magazine. There is a subject-verb agreement error in each sentence. Circle the errors, and then rewrite the advertisement correctly.

Cost Cuts Ltd	line 1
Cost Cuts Ltd have been working successfully in Hambridge	line 2
for seven years. Due to our recent expansion we has a	line 3
vacancy for a new trainee hair stylist. The successful	line 4
candidate are joining a thriving company and will have	line 5
excellent career opportunities. Training will be on the job,	line 6
with one day's release to attended Bridgwater College.	line 7
Your application must show that you has good GCSE results	line 8
in English and maths and that you is also willing to work	line 9
Saturdays and occasional evening shift. If you is genuinely	line 10
interested in training to be a hair stylist please contact	line 11
Sophie on 013423 760953.	line 12
Cost Cuts	line 13

Cost Cuts

F4 Using pronouns

This worksheet accompanies **pages 80–81** in the *Level 2 Skills Book*

Name _____ Date _____

1   Tick the boxes to show which of the following pairs of sentences are correct.

A ☐ **A** You need to walk the dogs because he is restless.

☐ **B** You need to walk the dogs because they are restless.

B ☐ **A** Mina asked Sally if she had remembered to bring the CD.

☐ **B** Mina asked Sally if they had remembered to bring the CD.

C ☐ **A** I paused and the silence strikes me.

☐ **B** I paused and the silence struck me.

D ☐ **A** As the sun came from behind a cloud the shadows disappeared.

☐ **B** As the sun came from behind a cloud the shadows disappear.

2   Circle any nouns that could be replaced with pronouns. Write the correct pronoun at the end of each sentence.

A   When Kermit forgot to visit his Grandma, Kermit felt guilty. _____

B   The car made an awful noise so the owner parked the car. _____

C   My friends and I were late so my friends and I missed the last bus home. _____

D   Parvati failed her driving text, but Parvati took the test again and passed. _____

E   Sheila liked the shoes because the shoes were bright red. _____

F   Joe kicked his ball over the fence and the neighbour gave the ball back to Joe. _____

3   The meaning of the pronouns in these sentences is not clear. Write down two possible meanings for each sentence. The first has been done for you.

A   Amy and Meera wore the same dress to the party, but because she got there first she felt that she should go and get changed and not herself.

■ Amy got to the party first, and felt that Meera should go and get changed.

■ Meera got to the party first and felt that Amy should go and get changed.

B   If the cat will not drink the milk because it is too cold, put it in the microwave for a few seconds.

_____

_____

C   Gail asked Padma's daughter to help her.

_____

_____

D   If the baby does not like cold milk, try warming it.

_____

_____

E   Most people who have written a book think that it is brilliant.

_____

_____

F5 Grammar test 1

This worksheet accompanies **pages 74–83** in the *Level 2 Skills Book*

Name _____ Date _____

Read the following letter and then answer the questions below.

Dear Sir,	line 1
I was shocked to see the proposed development plans for Charville.	line 2
I cannot even imagine the damage another 200 houses will cause	line 3
to our small town. Another 200 cars <u>meant</u> that we will face traffic	line 4
queues wherever we go. _____, the increased population will	line 5
place a huge strain on our schools. The shopkeepers may feel that	line 6
<u>he</u> will increase <u>his</u> profits, because of the extra customers, but I	line 7
think the shops will become so crowded that people will travel out of	line 8
town to the nearest superstores._____, I am concerned that	line 9
the play park in the centre of town will be so packed that nobody	line 10
will go to <u>the play park</u>.	line 11
Yours sincerely,	line 12
James McNab	line 13
James McNab	line 14

1 The underlined word on line 4 is incorrect. It should be:

A ☐ means   **B** ☐ will mean

2 Which of the following connectives would be appropriate for the gap in line 5?

A ☐ But   **B** ☐ Also

C ☐ Consequently **D** ☐ In conclusion

3 The words <u>he</u> and <u>his</u> need to be changed on lines 6 and 7. Which of the following choices would be most appropriate?

A ☐ she and her   **B** ☐ they and his

C ☐ they and their

4 Which of the following connectives would be most appropriate for the gap in line 9?

A ☐ However   **B** ☐ So   **C** ☐ In addition

5 Which of the following pronouns would be appropriate to replace <u>the play park</u> in line 11?

A ☐ them   **B** ☐ her   **C** ☐ it

F6 Grammar test 2

This worksheet accompanies **pages 74–83** in the *Level 2 Skills Book*

Name _____   Date _____

Read the following argument from someone who supports organic farming. Then answer the questions below.

Organic farming	line 1
Organic farming is farming that is carried out	line 2
without using any fertilisers or pesticides.	line 3
_____, organic farmers do not give their	line 4
livestock antibiotics. Pesticides and antibiotics can	line 5
both be passed on to the consumer so obviously	line 6
organically produced food <u>are</u> going to be healthier.	line 7
Scientific tests have actually shown that organically	line 8
grown vegetables contain more nutrients than non-	line 9
organic food.	line 10
Organic farmers are not only kinder to the	line 11
consumer; _____ also kinder to the land.	line 12
This means that we will be able to grow crops for	line 13
future generations. _____, organic farming	line 14
promotes bio-diversity which means that our	line 15
countryside supports a wider range of plants and	line 16
wild animals.	line 17

1 Which of the following connectives would be most appropriate for the gap on line 4?

A ☐ However   B ☐ Also

C ☐ Finally   D ☐ Consequently

2 The underlined word on line 7 is incorrect. It should be:

A ☐ is   B ☐ were

3 Which phrase would best fill the gap on line 12?

A ☐ we are   B ☐ they will

C ☐ they are   D ☐ it will

4 Which of the following connectives would be most appropriate to fill the gap on line 14?

A ☐ Eventually   B ☐ Despite this

C ☐ Possibly   D ☐ What is more

G Preparing for the test

(pages 84–93 in the Skills Book)

This section of the Teacher's Handbook contains worksheets aimed directly at students, including:

- advice about how to prepare for the test

- guidance on how to achieve optimum performance in the test

- a practice test with answers

- answers for this test that offer advice about how the students can use additional worksheets at the end of the section to revise question types that they have found difficult.

Each part of this section has been designed so that it can be photocopied for students.

G1 Top tips for the test

This section gives advice about how to prepare for the test, and how to approach the test on the day.

G2 How to tackle different kinds of question

This section gives examples of many of the question types that students are likely to face in the test. Explanations then clarify what each question is asking.

G3 Test vocabulary

This section contains typical test questions and explains any technical vocabulary that may give students problems.

G4 Tests

Section G4 presents six test questions on each of four passages. These 24 questions cover the main styles of questions that students are likely to encounter in the test.

G5 Test answers

Answers are provided for the tests in Sections G2 and G4. For each question, students are directed to similar question types that appear in worksheets in Section G6. In this way students can have further practice at question types that they have found difficult.

G6 Worksheets

Four additional worksheets are provided so that students can have even more test practice. These worksheets directly support the tests in Sections G2 and G4. Answers are provided Section G5.

Answers to worksheets

Answers are provided for the worksheets in Sections A to F.

G1 Top tips for the test

Preparing for the test

- Look back at everything you have been taught and revise everything thoroughly. Go back over any sections of the Skills Book that you found difficult, and do the practice tests in Section G4 and G6. Use the Hot Topics CD-ROM to help you revise grammar and punctuation.

- Make sure that you understand all of the technical vocabulary that is likely to appear in the test, e.g. style, grammar, tone, punctuation.

- Do the tests on the Practice Tests CD-ROM, and time yourself. This will help you:
  - understand how the paper is set out
  - be reminded about the different types of questions
  - learn how fast you have to work
  - see if there is anything you need to learn again.

- Revise with a friend, testing each other on aspects of the test specifications and discussing each other's answers.

- Start your revision early so that you will be able to bring any problems you have to the attention of your tutor, who can help you.

On the day of the test

- Make sure that you have everything you need, such as a pencil and an eraser, and leave behind what is not allowed, such as your mobile phone and your calculator.

- Listen carefully to what the invigilator has to say, and then read the instructions for the test carefully.

- Remember, for each question you must always choose only ONE answer from the four choices that you are given. Read all four carefully before making your choice.

- If you don't know the answer to a question try to work it out rather than guess. If you are unsure of your answer, mark it for review at the end of the test. No points are deducted for wrong answers so don't leave any blanks.

- Time your progress. Make sure that you have enough time to answer all of the questions with a few minutes to spare for checking. If you are taking the test on screen, you will be able to see how much time is remaining throughout the test. It is important to pace yourself.

- When you come to the end, check your answers for any mistakes before finishing the test.

G2 How to tackle different kinds of questions

Name _____   Date _____

All of the questions in the test are multiple-choice questions. You will be given four possible answers and you have to choose the ONE correct answer.

■ It is essential that you read each question very carefully so that you are sure what it is asking you.

■ You must read all of the possible answers and choose the option that best answers the question.

Questions 1–6 are about this extract from a health leaflet about marijuana.

> It is widely believed amongst teenagers that smoking marijuana is safe. *(line 1)*
> However, medical evidence clearly shows that smoking just one joint a day *(line 2)*
> can cause a wide range of serious medical problems. One horrifying finding *(line 3)*
> is that marijuana makes smokers less able to fight off infections and so *(line 4)*
> they are more likely to suffer from chest conditions such as pneumonia. *(line 5)*
> _____, it is felt that smoking marijuana can contribute to lung *(line 6)*
> cancer – we all know that smoking tobacco causes cancer, but there is four *(line 7)*
> times as much tar in marijuana as there is in tobacco, so what must a joint *(line 8)*
> be doing to the lungs. More significantly, there is some _____ that *(line 9)*
> smoking marijuana causes many people to suffer serious mental conditions *(line 10)*
> such as flashbacks, hallucinations, depression, and uncontrollable *(line 11)*
> aggression. So, while many people say that smoking marijuana helps *(line 12)*
> them to relax, with each joint that they smoke they are storing up serious *(line 13)*
> problems for the future. *(line 14)*

1 What is the main purpose of this text?

A ☐ to tell people some facts about marijuana

B ☐ to persuade people that smoking marijuana is dangerous

C ☐ to entertain

D ☐ to argue that teenagers are wrong about marijuana.

2 According to the text, which of the following is true?

A ☐ All teenagers smoke marijuana.

B ☐ Marijuana is safer than other drugs.

C ☐ There is less tar in tobacco than marijuana.

D ☐ Smoking less than one joint a day is safe.

Test tip

It would be possible to say that the text does all of these things. However, the *main* purpose is the most important one. Try each of the options as a title for the passage and see which one feels best.

Test tip

You will be asked questions about the factual details of a text. However, at first sight all of the options might sound right. Don't choose the first option that sounds right to you, because three of the options have been written to try to catch you out. Read all four carefully.

Name _____   Date _____

3 According to the text, what is the most serious consequence of smoking marijuana?

A ☐ It causes medical problems.

B ☐ It makes people less able to fight infections.

C ☐ It can contribute to lung cancer.

D ☐ It causes serious mental health problems.

Test tip

Smoking marijuana does everything mentioned in these four options. However, the question asked what is the *most serious* consequence. Look in the passage for words or phrases such as *mainly*, *most* and *even more serious*.

4 Which of the following words would best fill the gap in line 6?

A ☐ Also

B ☐ However

C ☐ Obviously

D ☐ Alternatively

Test tip

The options here are all words that are used to link ideas together logically. Try each word out in the gap and see which one links the sentence to the previous sentence in the way that seems most logical.

5 The correct spelling of the word missing in line 9 is:

A ☐ evidance

B ☐ evidense

C ☐ evedence

D ☐ evidence

Test tip

Questions about spelling always give you four options that are very similar. Use pens or pencils to hide three of the options so that you look at each option on its own. It is much easier to see that a word has been spelt incorrectly if you look at it on its own.

6 What piece of punctuation is missing in line 9?

A ☐ two commas

B ☐ an apostrophe of possession

C ☐ a question mark

D ☐ one comma

Test tip

You will be asked a question about punctuation. You need to learn how each of these pieces of punctuation works in a sentence. You also need to know about the apostrophe of abbreviation, and how to paragraph longer pieces of writing.

G3 Test vocabulary

You need to know exactly what the test questions are asking you to do. Here are some example questions with explanations of what the examiner expects.

1 The best word to **replace** 'potential' in line 4 is

A ☐ possible

B ☐ probable

C ☐ future

D ☐ ability.

This question is asking **what word means the same as** potential.

2 What **grammatical error** is there in line 8?

Grammatical errors are things like mistakes with tenses, or mistakes with verb-subject agreement.

3 Which phrase does not suit the **formal tone** of this extract?

You would expect a **formal tone** in a textbook or official letter: complete sentences; Standard English; difficult words. You would expect an **informal tone** in a note or an e-mail to a friend: abbreviations; incomplete sentences; simple words.

4 In this **draft document** there are a number of spelling errors.

When you write something and then check it carefully before copying out a final copy, the first version is a **draft**.

5 What is the best word to describe the **style** of this extract?

The **style** of a piece of writing refers to the way the writer has expressed himself or herself. For example, it might be formal, informal, amusing, persuasive, argumentative or objective, or might have more than one quality, for example, argumentative *and* objective, or informal *and* amusing.

6 Where is this extract most likely to have come from?

A ☐ a textbook

B ☐ a leaflet

C ☐ a newspaper article

D ☐ a poster.

This is asking you to consider **the form** of the extract. Look for headings, subheadings and pictures. Think about the font or fonts that have been used. Do the colours, or lack of colour, give you any clues? Finally, think carefully about the written style. Look for layout and linguistic features.

7 What **punctuation** error has been made in line 3?

You have learnt about elements of **punctuation** including: full stops to end sentences; commas to separate items in a list; commas to separate additional information in a sentence; apostrophes of abbreviation; apostrophes of possession; paragraphing.

8 What is the writer's **main aim** in this extract?

The writer will have more than one aim in a piece of writing. For example, they may want to persuade and entertain. The writer's main aim is what they **most** want to achieve in the piece of writing.

 Test 1

Name _____   Date _____

Questions 1–6 are based on this extract from an article about the pressure group Greenpeace.

A pressure group is a group of people organised in order to influence public opinion   line 1
and government decisions they are very important because they strive for ideals,   line 2
even when they employ illegal methods. Greenpeace is a high profile pressure group   line 3
which aims to protect the world's environment. Some of its greatest _____   line 4
have included persuading governments to implement a ban on toxic waste from   line 5
developed countries to less developed countries, and influencing bans on the   line 6
dumping of radioactive and industrial waste into the seas. However, their message   line 7
is that we can all make a _____ to protecting the environment. They argue   line 8
that the average person can help the environment by walking or using public   line 9
transport and washing cars the natural way – wait until it rains!   line 10

1 According to the text, what is a pressure group?

- **A** ☐ A group of people with the same interests.
- **B** ☐ A group of people who try to influence opinions.
- **C** ☐ A group that uses illegal methods to change the way people behave.
- **D** ☐ A group that wants to protect the environment.

2 According to the text, which of the following is true?

- **A** ☐ Only governments can save the environment.
- **B** ☐ The biggest threat to the environment is toxic waste.
- **C** ☐ Greenpeace is a high profile pressure group.
- **D** ☐ People shouldn't wash their cars.

3 The correct spelling of the word missing on line 4 is:

- **A** ☐ achievments
- **B** ☐ achievemants
- **C** ☐ achievements
- **D** ☐ achevements

4 Which of the following phrases best describes the tone of this text?

- **A** ☐ Informal and amusing.
- **B** ☐ Informative and formal.
- **C** ☐ Persuasive and balanced.
- **D** ☐ Argumentative and objective.

5 Which pieces of punctuation are missing on line 2?

- **A** ☐ Two commas, one after opinion and one after important.
- **B** ☐ A question mark after decisions and a capital letter for they.
- **C** ☐ A comma after decisions and a capital letter for government.
- **D** ☐ A full stop after decisions and a capital letter for they.

6 The correct spelling of the word missing on line 8 is:

- **A** ☐ contribution
- **B** ☐ cotrabution
- **C** ☐ contribushion
- **D** ☐ contrabushion

G4 Test 2

Name _____   Date _____

Questions 7–12 are based on this article from a history textbook.

> On 22nd November 1963 President Kennedy visited Dallas, Texas to   line 1
> encourage people to support him in the 1964 presidential elections.   line 2
> As his plane lands he was greeted by thousands of cheering people   line 3
> and the cheering continued as his motorcade made its way through   line 4
> the main streets of Dallas.   line 5
>
> The atmosphere of celebration was shattered at 12.30 p.m. when a   line 6
> shot rang out and Kennedy watched by millions on the television   line 7
> grabbed at his throat with both hands. A second shot rang out and   line 8
> Kennedy's head exploded. He was rushed to hospital but the attempt   line 9
> to save his life was _____.   line 10
>
> An ex-marine, Lee Harvey Oswald, was arrested for the murder of   line 11
> President Kennedy but before he was put on trial he was shot by   line 12
> Jack Ruby.   line 13

7 Which of the following would be the best title for this article?

A ☐ The mystery behind Kennedy's assassination

B ☐ Who was Jack Ruby?

C ☐ The assassination of President Kennedy

D ☐ Dallas, Texas

8 According to the article, how many bullets hit President Kennedy?

A ☐ none

B ☐ one

C ☐ two

D ☐ more than two

9 According to the article, which of the following is **not** correct?

A ☐ Jack Ruby killed Lee Harvey Oswald.

B ☐ President Kennedy was murdered in Dallas.

C ☐ Lee Harvey Oswald was found guilty of murdering President Kennedy.

D ☐ President Kennedy was popular in Dallas.

10 What grammatical error is there on line 3?

A ☐ greeted should be in the present tense.

B ☐ lands should be in the past tense.

C ☐ thousands should not be plural.

D ☐ people should be spelt peoples.

11 What additional punctuation is required on line 7?

A ☐ A full stop after television.

B ☐ Television should start with a capital letter.

C ☐ A full stop after throat.

D ☐ A comma after Kennedy and after television.

12 The correct spelling of the word missing on line 10 is:

A ☐ unsuccesful

B ☐ unsuccessfull

C ☐ unsuckcessful

D ☐ unsuccessful

Test 3

Name _____   Date _____

Questions 13–18 are based on the table below.

Subject	A*	A	B	C	D	E	F	G	U
English	4	20	27	32	11	5	1	0	0
Maths	4	10	20	22	23	14	3	3	0
Science	1	10	18	50	17	2	2	0	0
History	13	12	16	18	17	15	7	2	0
French	1	17	20	36	16	7	0	3	0

2006 GCSE results for English maths science history and French in a Somerset comprehensive school. Figures are _____ of students who sat each subject: English – 253; maths – 253; Science – 230; History – 169; French – 88.

13 How have the examination figures been presented?

A ☐ In a paragraph.

B ☐ In a table.

C ☐ As a graph.

D ☐ In a diagram.

14 According to the figures, which of the following is true?

A ☐ The same percentage of students got A* in maths and English.

B ☐ More students got an A grade in science than maths or English.

C ☐ The highest percentage of students achieved Grade C in history.

D ☐ Nobody achieved a Grade U in these five subjects.

15 Which of the following statements is incorrect?

A ☐ The most common grade across all five subjects was C.

B ☐ More students got A* or A grades in French than in science.

C ☐ 25% of students taking history got A* or A grades.

D ☐ The highest percentage of students achieved A*–C grades in English.

16 Which of the following would be the best title for the figures?

A ☐ Examination results for Somerset School

B ☐ Percentage of A* grades in a Somerset School

C ☐ Grades achieved in some subjects by percentage of entry

D ☐ Examinations are getting easier

17 What is the correct spelling of the missing word in the writing below the figures?

A ☐ purcentage

B ☐ percentige

C ☐ percentige

D ☐ percentage

18 In the explanation below the figures, which punctuation error has been made?

A ☐ Some of the subjects don't have capital letters.

B ☐ There should be an exclamation mark at the end of the sentence.

C ☐ There should be a full stop after results.

D ☐ Commas should have been used to separate the items in the list.

G4 Test 4

Name _____   Date _____

Questions 19–24 are based on the draft letter below.

> Dear Julie,   line 1
>
> Thank's ever so much for coming down to stay with me last week. I   line 2
> had an ace time. I hope you did too.   line 3
>
> The trip to London was brill. It's _____ how much shopping   line 4
> you can fit into three hours. Did you realise that I managed to get a   line 5
> new skirt two tops a pair of shoes and some tights – all for less than   line 6
> £100.   line 7
>
> _____, I've got to wait until August 'til I see you again. It's   line 8
> going to be boring living here with no-one of my own age, but still   line 9
> it's only three months' away. It'll gave me time to save up some cash   line 10
> for our next shopping trip! Miss U. Right back.   line 11
>
> Love,   line 12
>
> Sue   line 13

19 Which of the following words would most appropriately start line 8?

A ☐ So
B ☐ However
C ☐ Because
D ☐ Alternatively

20 On which lines has the apostrophe been used incorrectly?

A ☐ lines 1 and 4
B ☐ lines 4 and 7
C ☐ lines 8 and 9
D ☐ lines 2 and 10

21 What punctuation is missing from the sentence that begins on line 5 and goes on to line 7?

A ☐ Two commas to separate additional information.
B ☐ Commas to separate items in a list.
C ☐ A question mark at the end of the sentence.
D ☐ A capital letter at the beginning of shoes.

22 What is the correct spelling of the missing word on line 4?

A ☐ suprising
B ☐ surprising
C ☐ serprising
D ☐ surpricing

23 What grammatical error has been made on line 10?

A ☐ *me* should be *my*
B ☐ *cash* should be plural – *cashs*
C ☐ *gave* should be *give*
D ☐ *It'll* should be *It'd*

24 Which word has been spelt incorrectly in the last paragraph?

A ☐ *wait* should be *weight*
B ☐ *away* should be *aweigh*
C ☐ *some* should be *sum*
D ☐ *Right* should be *Write*

The two tables below give the answers to G2 and G4. They also tell you what type of question each of the questions in G2 and G4 is. If there are any question types that you find difficult, check the table on page 82 to find more questions of that type in G6 so that you can practise them.

G2 Answers

This is the answer. Tick if you got it right	This is the skill that the question is testing
1B ☐	Purpose
2C ☐	Factual detail
3D ☐	Factual detail
4A ☐	Connectives
5D ☐	Spelling
6C ☐	Punctuation

G4 Answers

This is the answer. Tick if you got it right	This is the skill that the question is testing
1B ☐	Factual detail
2C ☐	Factual detail
3C ☐	Spelling
4B ☐	Tone
5D ☐	Punctuation
6A ☐	Spelling
7C ☐	Title
8C ☐	Factual detail
9C ☐	Factual detail
10B ☐	Grammar
11D ☐	Punctuation
12D ☐	Spelling
13B ☐	Presentational features
14D ☐	Factual detail
15A ☐	Factual detail
16C ☐	Factual detail
17D ☐	Spelling
18D ☐	Punctuation
19A ☐	Connective
20D ☐	Punctuation
21C ☐	Punctuation
22B ☐	Spelling
23C ☐	Grammar
24D ☐	Spelling

G5 G6 worksheets and answers

Once you have completed sections G2 and G4, and checked your answers, look at the table on page 81 to find out if there are any skills you need to practise more. Then find those skills in the table below and look in the right-hand columns to find more questions of this type to give you further practice. The answers to these questions are in the table at the bottom of the page.

Where to find questions of a similar type in the G6 worksheets

Question type	Where to find more examples in G6	
	Worksheet	Question number
Title	G6D	1
Tone	G6C	1
Purpose	G6A	1
Presentational features	G6A	1
Factual details	G6B	1
	G6D	2
Connectives	G6A	2
Spelling	G6A	5
	G6B	3 and 4
	G6C	4 and 5
	G6D	3 and 4
Punctuation	G6A	4
	G6B	4
	G6D	5
Grammar	G6C	2

Table 4 G6 Answers

Worksheet G6A	Worksheet G6B	Worksheet G6C
1C ☐	1B ☐	1C ☐
2C ☐	2D ☐	2C ☐
3C ☐	3B ☐	3B ☐
4A ☐	4B ☐	4A ☐
5A ☐	5B ☐	5B ☐

Answers to Skills Book Section G Preparing for the test – G1

This is the answer. Tick if you got it right	This is the skill that the question is testing
1B ☐	Factual detail
2B ☐	Factual detail
3D ☐	Factual detail
4A ☐	Purpose
5A ☐	Purpose
6A ☐	Factual detail
7D ☐	Tone
8A ☐	Tone
9C ☐	Tone
10D ☐	Purpose
11A ☐	Presentational features
12B ☐	Grammar
13D ☐	Presentational features
14C ☐	Factual detail

Answers to Skills Book Section G Preparing for the test – G2

This is the answer. Tick if you got it right	This is the skill that the question is testing
1B ☐	Grammar
2A ☐	Grammar
3D ☐	Grammar
4B ☐	Spelling
5A ☐	Spelling
6C ☐	Punctuation
7D ☐	Punctuation
8C ☐	Punctuation
9D ☐	Connective
10C ☐	Grammar
11A ☐	Grammar
12C ☐	Grammar
13B ☐	Grammar
14C ☐	Grammar

G6 Worksheet A

Name _____   Date _____

Questions 1–5 are based on the text below.

> Hawkehurst is an ancient village that is recorded in the   line 1
> Doomsday Book. In 1086 the population was only 27 but   line 2
> today there are over 1000 residents. Most of the residents   line 3
> are _____ in agriculture, with some relying heavily   line 4
> on seasonal work. _____ the community is so small it   line 5
> cannot support it's own school and so children have to travel   line 6
> by bus to the local market town of Stow-on-the-Wold for   line 7
> primary and secondary education.   line 8
>
> Hawkehurst is a close community with a thriving social life   line 9
> based on traditional rural activities. The Rose and Crown's   line 10
> two skittle teams meet twice a week, and its darts team once   line 11
> a week. The church, All Saints, runs coffee mornings jumble   line 12
> sales quiz nights and a playschool.   line 13

1 Where is this text most likely to be from?

A ☐ A holiday brochure

B ☐ A newspaper article

C ☐ An encyclopaedia

D ☐ A letter.

2 Which of the following words would most appropriately fill the gap in line 5?

A ☐ So

B ☐ However

C ☐ Because

D ☐ Luckily

3 Which of the following statements is correct?

A ☐ Rose and Crown's should be Rose and Crowns'.

B ☐ Rose and Crown's should not have an apostrophe.

C ☐ Rose and Crown's is correctly punctuated.

D ☐ Rose and Crown's should be Rose's and Crown's.

4 What punctuation is missing from lines 12–13?

A ☐ Commas to separate items in a list

B ☐ An exclamation mark at the end of the sentence

C ☐ A dash between jumble and sales

D ☐ A capital letter for playschool.

5 The correct spelling of the word missing in line 4 is:

A ☐ employed

B ☐ imployed

C ☐ emploid

D ☐ emplloyed

G6 Worksheet B

Name _____   Date _____

Questions 1–5 are based on the draft text below.

Dear Governors, — line 1

I hope to persuade you that school uniform was a bad thing and should be abandoned. Although many parents support school uniform, I am sure that they would change their minds if they knew all of the facts. — line 2 / line 3 / line 4 / line 5

We all know the arguments about cost, and the arguments about lack of style and lack of comfort. This issue is been raised _____ in the past. However, for me the most damning argument against school uniform is its role in stifling independent thought. The teachers want us all dressed the same because they believe we will behave ourselves and work hard. However, along with everyone _____ the same comes everyone thinking the same. — line 6 / line 7 / line 8 / line 9 / line 10 / line 11 / line 12 / line 13

A successful education should encourage independent thought but the school uniform discourages it. Please change your minds about school uniform and allow our minds to become less uniform. — line 14 / line 15 / line 16 / line 17

Yours sincerely, — line 18

John Groats — line 19

1 Which of the following words best describes the tone of this text?

- **A** ☐ informal
- **B** ☐ persuasive
- **C** ☐ objective
- **D** ☐ humorous

2 Which lines contain grammatical errors?

- **A** ☐ lines 3 and 8
- **B** ☐ lines 5 and 10
- **C** ☐ lines 1 and 5
- **D** ☐ lines 2 and 7

3 Which of the following words would best replace stifling on line 9?

- **A** ☐ boiling
- **B** ☐ stopping
- **C** ☐ airless
- **D** ☐ promoting

4 The correct spelling of the word missing on line 8 is:

- **A** ☐ unsuccesfully
- **B** ☐ unsuccessfully
- **C** ☐ unsuccessfuly
- **D** ☐ unsuckcessfully

5 The correct spelling of the word missing on line 12 is:

- **A** ☐ behaveing
- **B** ☐ behaving
- **C** ☐ behaiving
- **D** ☐ behaiveing

G6 Worksheet C

Name _____   Date _____

Questions 1–5 are based on the text below.

> HMS Victory was Admiral Lord Nelson's flagship during   line 1
> the Battle of Trafalgar, in 1805. It was on this ship that   line 2
> Nelson was fatally shot. Today HMS Victory can be visited in   line 3
> Portsmouth and it is possible to see how our brave sailors   line 4
> lived at the _____ of the 19th century.   line 5
>
> The impressive Victory is 227 feet long and 52 feet wide, and   line 6
> it took 2000 oak trees to build her. There are four huge masts   line 7
> which together carry 4 acres of sails. Most of the sailors'   line 8
> lived below deck amongst the 102 cannons. During the day   line 9
> they would eat in-between the cannons and at night they   line 10
> would sleep in their hammocks above the cannons. Today it   line 11
> is possible to _____ the cramped, dark conditions and   line 12
> wonder how people spent years living in these conditions.   line 13
>
> Open all year round, HMS Victory is ideal for all the family to line 14
> experience.   line 15

1 Which of the following would be the most appropriate title for this text?

A ☐ HMS Victory

B ☐ Battle of Trafalgar

C ☐ Conditions aboard ships in the eighteen hundreds

D ☐ Go back over 200 years and learn about Britain's most famous warship

2 How many trees were felled to build HMS Victory?

A ☐ 227

B ☐ 1805

C ☐ 2000

D ☐ 102

3 The correct spelling of the word missing on line 5 is:

A ☐ begining

B ☐ beginning

C ☐ beggining

D ☐ begineng

4 The correct spelling of the word missing on line 12 is:

A ☐ experience

B ☐ experiense

C ☐ ecsperience

D ☐ ecsperience

5 What punctuation error appears in the sentence on lines 8–9?

A ☐ There should not be a full stop after cannons.

B ☐ sailors' does not need an apostrophe.

C ☐ deck should have a capital letter.

D ☐ cannons should have an apostrophe.

Answers to worksheets

A1

1 **e-mail:** abbreviations; words missed out; friendly tone; first person ('I've')
2 **formal letter:** addresses; salutation ('Dear Sir'); formal language; first person ('I have')
3 **newspaper report:** headline; personal details; emotive language (e.g. attractive, riotous); third person ('she')

A2

A **Formal letter accepting an invitation:** Paragraphs
B **Memo explaining procedure:** Numbering; Bullet points; Bold or italic text
C **E-mail to a friend:** Paragraphs
D **Newspaper article:** Heading; Subheadings; Paragraphs
E **Information leaflet:** Heading; Subheadings; Bullet points; Paragraphs; Bold or italic text
F **Advertisement in a magazine:** Heading; Bold or italic text

A3

Skimming means looking over a text quickly to find out what it's about.

Scanning means quickly running your eyes across the page to find the answer to a particular question.

Close reading means reading a text carefully so you can really understand it.

1 scanning
2 skimming
3 skimming
4 scanning
5 close reading
6 close reading

A4

1 A
2 A
3 B
4 B
5 C
6 C

Answers to worksheets

A5

1 C
2 A
3 B
4 C
5 C
6 A

A6

1 important
2 quickly
3 extraordinary
4 progress
5 achievement
6 tribute

B1

A Information leaflet/presentational features: headlines; subheadings; illustrations; columns.

B Advertisement/language features: addressed specifically to the reader; may break grammatical rules; persuasive language – extensive use of adjectives, adverbs; superlatives; imperatives.

C Newspaper report/presentational features: headlines; subheadings; illustrations, columns.

D Letter/language features: formal language; carefully structured.

B2

A Front cover of magazine

(i) language features: informal language; slang; aimed directly at target audience;

(ii) presentational features: bright colours; range of informal fonts; cartoons; eye-catching illustrations photographs.

B Homepage of website

(i) language features: formal language; aimed directly at target audience;

(ii) presentational features: formal colours; range of formal fonts; photographs; hyperlinks.

C Page from a textbook

(i) language features: formal language; technical language; third person

(ii) presentational features: black and white; range of formal fonts; diagrams.

B3

1 D
2 B
3 B
4 D
5 A
6 C

B4

1 C
2 B
3 C
4 B
5 A
6 C

B5

1 D
2 A
3 A
4 D
5 C
6 B

B6

This sheet is a revision aid.

C1

1 **A** Purpose: To persuade people to recycle.
  B Audience: Teenagers.
2 **A** Purpose: To describe a sombre scene.
  B Audience: Adults.
3 **A** Purpose: Persuade school students that they should complain about their uniform.
  B Audience: School students.

C2

1 A
2 C
3 C
4 B
5 D

Answers to worksheets

C3

1 A
2 B
3 C

C4

1 A
2 B
3 B
4 D
5 A

C5

1 B
2 C
3 D
4 D
5 C

C6

1 C
2 B
3 D
4 C

D1

1 **A** echoes
   B knives
   C glasses
   D countries
   E calves
   F leaves
2 parties, pencils, dictionaries, churches, gases, halves, pianos, foxes
3 photoes, photos
   babys, babies
   penciles, pencils
   dictionarys, dictionaries
   shelfs, shelves
   ladys, ladies

D2

1. weighting, waiting
   male, mail
   male, mail
   for, four
   won, one
   hole, whole
   sum, some
   too, two
2. **A** steal
   B sauce
   C wore
   D would
   E towed
   F piece
3. reign, pane, storey, quay, bawl, herd

D3

1. replay, disappear, underground, overweight, impolite, unwanted, invisible
2. **A** inexperienced
   B inaccurate
   C unexpected
   D indecisive
   E impolite
   F impossible
3. re – again; mis – wrong; tri – three; pre – before; un – not; post – after

D4

1. **A** running
   B sunny
   C pumped
   D travelling
   E treated
2. headed, qualified, running, studied, dominated, travelled, benefiting, retiring, Organising, successful

D5

1. B
2. C
3. C
4. A
5. C
6. A
7. B

D6

1 A
2 A
3 C
4 A
5 C
6 B
7 C
8 B

E1

1 **A** Question
   B Command
   C Statement
   D Exclamation.
2 **A** Do you think that Razorlight's new CD is better than their first one?
   B I must remember to send a card to my friend in France.
   C Help! Help!
   D I would like to go to Nottingham University next year.
   E Would you like to come to town with me tonight?
   F Just sit there and shut up!
3 **a)** A
   b) C
   c) B
   d) C

E2

1 **A** To separate items in a list.
   B To separate out clauses.
   C To separate out additional information.
   D To separate out additional information.
   E To separate items in a list.
   F To separate clauses.
2 **A** Today I went to town and bought three bright shirts, a pair of brown shoes, a blue and red tie and a box of handkerchiefs.
   B Yesterday, after I finished all of my work, I went to the cinema.
   C Although Harriet was hungry, she refused to eat because she was on a diet.
   D To get to Taunton from here you need to go down this road for two miles, turn left at the crossroads, continue for about a hundred yards, turn left at the t-junction then continue for about four miles. It's easy.

E It was a dark night, the darkest night for ages, and Dean was scared.

F Lucy spilt beer down her dress, completely ruining it.

G Jo bought some fresh fruit from the supermarket, then she went straight home.

H When I was younger, much younger, I lived in Holland.

I In my opinion, for what it's worth, everyone should try to save some money every month.

J My favourite meal is rib-eye steak, sauté potatoes, mushrooms, battered onions and peas.

E3

1   Should've
     Could've
     We're
     You're
     Isn't
     It's
     Couldn't
     Wouldn't

2   **A** Jane's sister was going to visit today.

  B It's freezing outside.

  C Bill crashed his car because the car's tyres were so worn.

  D The men's changing room is being decorated.

  E The brothers' bedroom was really too small for them.

  F The English teachers' office was designed to fit them all in.

  G Calvin's and Robert's exercise books have gone missing.

E4

1   C
2   D
3   B
4   D

E5

1   C
2   C
3   B
4   C

Answers to worksheets

E6

1 C
2 A
3 C
4 C
5 A

F1

1 Sequencing: First; Next
   Cause and effect: Therefore; As a result
   Contrasting: However; Meanwhile
   Illustrating: For example; For instance
   Emphasising: Above all; indeed
   Concluding: Finally; Ultimately

2 **1** First
   2 Next
   3 For example
   4 However
   5 Indeed

F2

1 **1** have
   2 had
   3 did
   4 enjoyed
   5 didn't
   6 visited
   7 look forward
   8 hope

2 **a)** A
   b) C
   c) B
   d) C

F3

1 **A** are
   B have
   C is
   D will
   E are
   F is

Literacy Teacher's Handbook Level 2 © Edexcel Limited 2006

2 Cost Cuts Ltd has been working successfully in Hambridge for seven years. Due to our recent expansion we have a vacancy for a new trainee hair stylist. The successful candidate is joining a thriving company and will have excellent career opportunities. Training will be on the job, with one day's release to attend Bridgwater College.

Your application must show that you have good GCSE results in English and Maths and that you are also willing to work Saturdays and occasional evening shifts. If you are genuinely interested in training to be a hair stylist please contact Sophie on 013423 760953.

F4

1 **a)** B
   b) A
   c) B
   d) A
2 **A** Kermit : he
   B car : it
   C my friends and I : we
   D Parvati : she
   E the shoes : they
   F the ball : it
3 B Put the cat in the microwave; put the milk in the microwave.
   C Gail asked Padma's daughter to help Gail; Gail asked Padma's daughter to help Padma.
   D Warm the milk; warm the baby.
   E People think that it is brilliant to write novels; people think that the novels they write are brilliant.

F5

1 B
2 B
3 C
4 C
5 C

F6

1 B
2 A
3 C
4 D